A Garden
of Quilts

Mary
Elizabeth
Johnson

Oxmoor
House®

*To the memory of my mother, Helen Louise Pearson
Johnson (1919-1971), who taught me that, no matter
how busy you are, there is always time for beauty.*

Mother's Patchwork Quilt

*I see my mother's patchwork quilt
   upon my bed upstairs,
And stitched into each tiny piece
   are all her love and cares.*

*I see my sisters' dresses,
   a piece of mother's skirt,
A bit of brother's rompers,
   a square of daddy's shirt.*

*I see her work-worn hands
   by fading evening light,
Piecing tiny diamonds
   far into the night.*

*A square of yellow,
   bits of pink,
Strips of blue and red.
   Oh! I am so proud
To spread it on my bed.*

*May I cherish that old quilt
   a thing of beauty rare,
For I saw my mother stitching
   love in every square.*

Winnie Wilcox Garner

Copyright 1984 Oxmoor House, Inc.
Book Division of Southern Progress Corporation
P.O. Box 2463, Birmingham, Alabama 35201

Library of Congress Catalog Number: 84-60630
ISBN: 0-8487-0629-3
Manufactured in the United States of America
First Edition, Second Printing

Pansy Wreath *(preceding page)*
Being quilted by Patty Cox Wilcox;
Robertsdale, Alabama.
Quilt pieced and assembled by her
mother-in-law, Rebena Elizabeth
Ard Wilcox Boyington, 1980.
(See Suppliers for pattern source.)

Purple Iris *(contents page)*
Owned and made by Beulah Wilcox
Wigley; Robertsdale, Alabama;
1946.
Finished size of quilt: 76″ x 93″.
(See Suppliers for pattern source.)

Contents

Flower Quilts: Perennial Favorites

"And purple all the ground with vernal flowers,
Bring the rathe primrose that forgotton dies,
The tufted crow-toe, and pale jessamine,
The white pink, and the pansy freked with jet,
The glowing violet,
The musk-rose, and the well-attir'd woodbine,
With cowslips wan that hang the pensive head,
And every flower that embroidery wears."

John Milton

It is impossible to imagine a world without flowers. The most arid of urban landscapes, the driest of deserts, the most frozen of Arctic tundra is brightened with some kind of blossom at some point during the year. A vast body of poetry attests to the fact that man cannot remain unmoved in the face of such beauty; even the most melancholy of poets have praised the effect of flowers upon the observer!

Flowers have been the inspiration for artists since the cave painters. Van Gogh painted lively bouquets of sunflowers to brighten his garret in Paris; try to imagine the still life paintings of the Old Masters like Rembrandt without their lilies and tulips. Think, too, of the Jacobean embroideries full of fanciful flowers and fat buds ready to pop open — surely what Milton was referring to in his poetry. The Jacobean works were no doubt influenced by the publication of tediously carved woodcuts of rare herbs and plants. (Many have been reissued, at least in part, by modern publishers, and are an excellent source for modern designers.)

A distinct oriental feeling of simplicity and purity of form is achieved in *Japanese Lily* by Sue McCarter of Charlotte, North Carolina.

A fabulous garden of poppies and irises grows in *Art Nouveau,* a commissioned piece by Pauline Burbidge; Nottingham, England.

Three hundred years later, flowers were the main inspiration for the Art Nouveau movement, so beautifully represented in a one-of-a-kind design by Pauline Burbidge (see photos above). In the intervening years, flowers had been an important part of the fine embroideries and tapestries of Elizabethan needlework, all the rage of Victoriana, and the inspiration for countless designers in all media.

Quilters, of course, are inspired by the same things that motivate painters and stitchery designers, although there is often more sentiment involved in a quilt design. During the great exploration of the West, the three most treasured items in the covered wagons were the Bible, springs or seeds from favorite flowering plants, and the woman's quilt patterns. When the many references to flowers in the Bible are combined with the incredible variety of native flowers encountered on those travels,

it's no wonder that there are more flower quilts than any other kind. There's hardly a blossom, large or small, that has escaped the quilter's notice! Some have been realistically rendered; others are so abstract they become a puzzle.

The appeal of flower quilts continues undiminished to this day; contemporary designers draw as much delight from floral motifs as did our ancestors. The variety of flower quilts is astonishing; it is impossible to count them all. One small variation on a standard pattern produces a new "hybrid" with a name of its own. Sometimes it seems there are almost as many flower quilts as there are flowers!

We welcome you into our garden and invite you to enjoy some old favorites as well as some new hybrids. Get out your needle and transplant them into your very own garden of quilts!

The Garden Changes with Time

"A garden is a lovesome thing—God wot!
Rose plot,
Fringed pool,
Fern grot—
The veriest school
Of peace; and yet the fool
Contends that God is not.—
Not God in gardens! When the sun is cool?
Nay, but I have a sign!
'Tis very sure God walks in mine."

Thomas Edward Brown

Fashions and popular tastes change as time passes, and those changes affect every aspect of our lives, including what we grow in our garden of quilts. Those fabulous flowers that quiltmakers have stitched into bouquets of beauty have not been picked out of thin air! They are the result of the same influences that affect the designs on china, wallpaper, furniture, and fabrics.

The most influential forces in quilt design have been the economy, the ease of communication with other communities or countries, what was visible out the back door, and what other people were doing (things don't change much!). These forces can be seen in the very

A Look at 1850 (opposite): All three of these quilt patterns were popular in 1850. From left: *Winter Tulip*, 1850; *Oak Leaf and Acorn*, (owned by Wallace Johnson, Franklin, Alabama) made in 1950 from an 1850 pattern; *Carolina Lily*, 1850. All are from Alabama, and the house is the Carlen House, Museum of the City of Mobile, Alabama, built in 1842. Pattern and description for *Winter Tulip* on page 148.

earliest flower quilts which show the influence of "making do" with the very limited materials at hand. Early quilts also show a great deal of local influence — quilters stitched what they saw. As communication with other communities and the Old World improved and times became more prosperous, flowered chintzes were imported and became an important part of quilt making. On the other hand, some communities deliberately kept themselves shut away from the modernization of society, and their quilts reflect this isolation.

It is generally accepted that quilt designs had a much more individual quality before the increasing availability of books and periodicals such as *Godey's Lady's Book*, which began to encourage a homogeneity of taste and standards, albeit innocently. The advent of kits and printed patterns in the late 1930s also contributed to a sameness of design in flower quilts, but they did get people quilting again after a war and an economic depression. These same four forces continue today to affect our outstanding contemporary designers. Each successive generation of quilters has a larger and larger body of work from which to draw when doing their own designing. Like a well-tended garden that grows more beautiful with each passing year, so, too, do our quilts reflect the beauty of their heritage.

The Oldest Quilt, a 1750s homespun appliqué coverlet contains many different kinds of flowers on a checkerboard background of red, blue and brown. The sunflower is easily recognizable, and the heart-shaped leaves of some of the other plants suggest violets. Made in Connecticut from wool, the quilt measures 65½" x 76". (Courtesy of The Baltimore Museum of Art.)

The Ann Robinson Spread gives us a look at the popular floral motifs of 1813 and 1814. Tulips were a favorite, gathered as they are here into five cornucopias and two bouquets. The profusion of leaves are fashioned into wreaths and laurel branches, and sprout from two trees. There are five-petaled and eight-petaled flowers, poinsettias, and some rather strange fiery-looking plants. The quilt measures 95" x 100".
(Courtesy of The Shelburne Museum.)

6

The Stenciled Quilt is as beautiful as it is rare. This quilt is very special because it is from Natchez, Mississippi, not New England, and is one of the only known Southern stenciled quilts. It was made by Caroline Lucinda Bayles sometime between 1823 and 1830. The rose was by far the favorite flower to stencil, and although Caroline has some rose shapes in her quilt, she also has asters, violets, trumpet vines, peonies, lilies, peaches, strawberries, and grapes. Her colors, lovely pale yellows and pinks combined skillfully with a dark blue and green, are strikingly different from the familiar red and green of other stenciled quilts.

(Quilt courtesy of the Dallas Historical Society; Information from "The Bayles Stenciled Quilt," Diane Church "Uncoverings 1983," The American Quilt Study Group 1984; Mill Valley, California.)

Lattice Flower Baskets combines fruit and flowers into woven baskets, typical of the period. Flowers appear to be lilies, roses, bridal wreath, morning glory, and maybe stock or delphinium. The running strawberry vine used between the baskets is particularly delicate and beautiful. The silk quilt is from Baltimore and was made by Mrs. Mary Jane Green Masan in 1845. It measures 87" x 94".
(Courtesy of The Smithsonian Institution.)

Three Pennsylvania German quilts reflect the motifs dear to folk artists of that area in the early 1800s. Legends and superstitions abounded concerning the magical properties of certain symbols — some were said to protect the house or barn from lightning, others from witches or evil spirits. As time passed, the symbols became prized more for their decorative properties than for any magical associations, but still the tulip with its three petals represented the Holy Trinity and the heart symbolized love and joy. Clear reds, yellows, bright blues, and greens were the favored colors. Quilters naturally adopted the folk art motifs as their own and produced equally vibrant and wonderful designs, although religious restrictions sometimes

prevented the application of these motifs to the front side of the quilt. A quilt of Amish Bars is sometimes found on the back of designs like *Spider Lily* or *Tulip Cross!*

Tulip Cross, or *Tulip and Princess Feather,* c. 1865, from the collection of Dick and Marti Michell; Atlanta, Georgia; 84″ x 84″.
Pattern and description on page 150.

Tulip and Heart, c. 1885, from the collection of Dick and Marti Michell; Atlanta, Georgia; 78″ x 90″.

Spider Lily or *Snowflake*, c. 1880, from the collection of Rick and Mary Grunbaum; Dallas, Texas; 88½″ x 88½″. Pattern and description on page 152.

9

Botanical Spread, from Connecticut, exhibits the Victorian love of natural forms in a way that would not be likely later, as the Victorians gradually lost all sense of restraint and began to heavily embellish their designs, making them almost indecipherable. The 26 different plants and flowers in this breath-taking summer spread appear to be randomly placed, but on examination we see a repetition of motifs balancing the overall design. This 94″ x 96″ spread seems to be a diary or record of treasured botanical motifs. It's almost as though "J.S." decided to record as many forms of plant life as she could by using appliqué rather than pressing flowers between the pages of a book as was popular in 1868.

(Courtesy of the Shelburne Museum.)

Victorian Moss Rose typifies the crazy quilt, that curious needlework fad of the late 19th century. The squares display various interpretations of the moss rose. Subordinate flowers and buds are worked in the surrounding borders and in corner blocks. Although the Victorian crazy quilt is criticized as sloppily sentimental, it is a true expression of its times. All sorts of special fabrics and ribbons were used — pieces from wedding and mourning dresses and bits of men's ties. And because the embroidery forms original stitchery pictures of everyday items, these quilts are wonderful pieces of American folk art.

From the collection of Dick and Marti Michell.

Early Thirties Appliqué appears to be a series of single theme designs. These series were extremely popular features of publications of the day, and some of the best known were by Ruby McKim and Nancy Cabot. This quilt is typical of the genre, portraying, as it does, different flowers in too-precious little arrangements. Morning glories form a wreath, crocuses are growing in a pot, pansies and roses are tied into bouquets with embroidery to look like ribbons (a holdover from the popular outline embroidery of the last quarter of the 19th century), and the most exotic of the lot, the water lily, is placed in the center of the quilt.

From the collection of Dick and Marti Michell.

Five quilts from Rose Kretsinger (1886 to 1963) take your breath away! Sharp students of quilting will remember that *Orchid Wreath* was also worked by Charlotte Jane Whitehill, whose work can be seen in the Denver Art Museum's *Quilts and Coverlets*. Ms. Whitehill's work is equally outstanding. She and Mrs. Kretsinger were contemporaries, and it is believed that Ms. Whitehill bought patterns from Mrs. Kretsinger. Their quilts were not identical, even when they used the same design. Each one marked the quilting design onto her quilt top, and someone else did the actual stitching. This was a common practice of the time, but Rose Kretsinger would often later add trapunto to already-quilted pieces. An interesting sidelight to the relationship between the two women is that Ms. Whitehill, in her job as a traveling insurance agent, would search her territory for different green fabrics for each of them to use as a supplement to the ubiquitous "30s Green" that seemed to be the only green color available.

Calendula (above right), 89" x 89½"; finished in 1940.

Oriental Poppy (right), 86" x 86¼"; date unknown.

Orchid Wreath (above) is believed to be her own design, inspired by a poster of orchids in an ice cream parlour. Her daughter saw the poster and wanted a quilt of orchids; this was the result. *Orchid Wreath,* 91½″ x 91″; sometime between 1925 and 1950.

Rose Tree (above), 87″ x 88″; finished between 1925 and 1950.

Paradise Garden (right) is an example of a traditional pattern taken from a book of the day, *Quilts; Their Story And How To Make Them,* by Marie Webster. Mrs. Kretsinger added her own interpretation to it to produce a true masterpiece. *Paradise Garden,* 93″ x 94½″; finished in 1945.

Kretsinger Quilts at the Spencer Museum of Art; Lawrence, Kansas.

Whitehill Quilts at the Denver Art Museum; Denver, Colorado.

Botanic Series I (left) is a bright little flower garden of pieced blossoms based on the Log Cabin design unit, measuring 47″ x 68″. The diagonal rows of blossoms in solid color fabrics create the sensation of lively movement. The maker thinks of it as a "Botanic Postcard."
Designed and made by Virginia Randles; Athens, Ohio; 1981.

Spring Quilt (below left) is a joyful profusion of favorite flowers, with the wonderful addition of birds, butterflies, ladybugs, and a "lucky old sun" with nothing to do but shine on this beauty all day!
Designed by Lesly-Claire Greenberg. Made as a group effort by the Vienna, Virginia Quilters of America Unlimited; 1979.

Williamsburg Gardens (below right) was inspired by a formal herb garden in the restored historic village. Bricks outline neat beds of flowering plants, and a gravel pathway connects the growing beds. The grayed greens of sage, thyme and rosemary are perfectly captured, as are the wonderful tiny blossoms typical of herbs.
Designed and made by Mary Lou Smith; Wilbraham, Massachusetts; 1983.

Grow Your Own Flower Quilts

"It has taken me half a lifetime merely to find out what is best worth doing, and a good slice out of another half to puzzle out the ways of doing it."

Gertrude Jekyll

A successful flower quilt must have a seed of inspiration, must be fertilized with creativity and weeded with discipline! When you say to yourself, "I sure would like to make a quilt that captures the way those hollyhocks stand against that picket fence," the seed is planted. The fertilizing starts when you begin looking around for a good hollyhock pattern. You begin doodling hollyhocks and pickets on your grocery list, and you can't seem to see anything but hollyhock colors when you go into the fabric store. The weeding comes in when you must decide how you are going to actually execute in fabric what you've pictured in your mind's eye. And, just as each season for a gardener is filled with hope, so it is with the "gardener" who works in fabric! The quilt that's in the planning stages is the best ever, for past mistakes are either forgotten or believed conquered.

Breaking Ground

Some people will want to know, "Where does the inspiration come from?" Aside from the obvious answer of live, growing flowers, there are seed catalogs and garden books, both excellent for their true-to-life representations of flowers. Magazines and, of course, books contain flower quilt patterns, and manufacturers of commercial patterns have many flower designs. You can copy old quilts (more about that later!), and you can look at the many items which are decorated with a flower motif—china, wallpaper, fabric, furniture, almost anything. Inevitably, you will say to yourself, "Now that's it, that's what I want, but I want the center to be a little larger, and I want it to be yellow instead of red." Now you are starting to fertilize and weed your seed of inspiration. Sometimes the inspiration is followed almost immediately by the creativity!

So often people say, "I'm just not creative — I just can't do anything; I can't even draw a straight line." What is really being said is, "I'm afraid to try to do anything, because it may not be perfect." Don't let fear or nervousness about your performance keep you from trying something—you should be afraid of not trying. Almost all of the quilts in this book were made by women who had to stretch themselves just a little bit to see if they could do something a little better than the last time, something a little more original. There is nothing like the feeling of personal triumph that comes from conquering that fear of trying something new. No person on this earth is without creativity of some kind, and if you are reading this now, you have the creativity within yourself to design your very own flower quilt.

One thing to remember is that you aren't working alone. Thank goodness quilters still follow the time-honored tradition of swapping information. Because of the ease of communication and the casual regard we now have for travel, it's almost like we are all participating in a continuous, gigantic, nationwide quilting bee. We're producing thousands of new quilts and, at the same time, working to preserve the quilts of our foremothers. You can join this group anytime you want and get on the grapevine of shared information. You will find people who will discuss almost any problem you have, including how to find time to quilt! Quilters are like gardeners in that the struggles they encounter in producing the perfect quilt or the perfect garden make for hours of great conversation. You will find experts on color, piecing, appliqué and on the history of quilting; you'll learn of sources for all kinds of fabric, templates, batting, quilt frames, and esoteric equipment; you'll be aware of where and when the big seminars and markets are being held. Join a group! Enter a quilt show! Participate! You will gain strength and confidence from your sister quilters. Nobody works well in a vacuum — you need input and support. Go out and get it!

Don't overlook the value of commercial sources. Remember, many of the best designers in the country work for pattern and kit manufacturers. You can learn from their expertise, especially when you are just starting out. Magazine and book publications also provide wonderful teaching experiences for the beginner, as well as challenges for the experienced quilter. One successful designer said, "I saw a peony pattern in *Quilter's Newsletter* several years ago and liked the basic block, but I came up with my own way of setting it together, and my own border design." It's sort of like buying a sprouted plant instead of a packet of seeds; it's a little further along, but you still have to put it in the garden for it to grow and flourish. Be grateful for your resources and use them, but be careful not to violate copyrights. If you make a flower quilt using a kit or commercial pattern and later somebody wants to publish your quilt, be certain to ask permission from your commercial source, and see that it is credited. Not only does this keep everybody happy, but it also documents quilts. Our granddaughters and great-granddaughters will appreciate us even more for it!

Formulate a Plan

Part of the creative process is planning the overall appearance of the quilt. Just as a gardener must know how each plant will look and what size it will be when it reaches maturity, you must decide how many different types of blocks you are going to use in your quilt, or if, indeed, you plan to use blocks. You may prefer a medallion quilt, but even so, the same

types of decisions must be reached. What will the basic block look like? How many flowers will be in each block? How will they fit together? Will they form an unexpected secondary design if they're set without sashing, as Helen Rose found with *Pink Dogwood* (page 36)? Her unplanned secondary design turned out to be a lagniappe, but you can't count on being so fortunate. Plan your quilt on graph paper, and sketch in every detail of one section, perhaps in a large scale, and you may see the pattern differently.

While you're planning the quilt on graph paper, you will realize that, again just like a gardener, you have to decide if you want a formal arrangement around a dominant center of interest such as in *Mississippi Springtime* (page 37); or if you want a bed of one single flower, such as the wonderful windblown look of our cover quilt (also shown on page 55). And, as a flower gardener carefully chooses and places plants according to their size, texture, and color, so you will choose the motifs for your blocks, borders, binding and backing to make a harmonious whole. You even have the option of designing your quilt like one of those wonderful English gardens which features a perfectly smooth grassy lawn (the center of the quilt), surrounded by wide beds of flowering plants (multiple borders).

A masterpiece of advance plannning is shown in *Figure 1*. The maker of the quilt decided to use a central medallion made from a printed cotton. The center features the Tree of Life and urns of flowers. She filled in the corners with block patchwork cut from flowered fabric and added an inner border of Flying Geese, breaking it at the corners to accommodate bedposts. An unpatterned section was added at the top where the bed pillows were to lie; no doubt they were put in a separate sham or pillow cover. A ruffled skirt was delightfully embellished with swags, nosegays, and bows which break gracefully at the corners. A triangle border and silk fringe finishes the skirt. It is generally accepted that many quilts were finished with wide ruffles like this, but the ruffles either wore out or were removed when the quilt was placed on a

different bed. It may be an idea worth incorporating again into modern quilts. Many people make a dust ruffle to match their quilt anyway, and this would keep the piece together and make it unique. This quilt was intelligently thought out, first of all to fit a specific bed, and secondly to ensure harmony among all the components.

Figure 1. Quilt by Mary Johnston; possibly North Carolina; English cotton fabrics; signed and dated 1793. Size, 80″ x 97″.
(Courtesy of The Henry Francis du Pont Winterthur Museum.)

Make Your Selections

A case could be made for designing a quilt completely backwards from the approach just described. Some will argue that the basic unit of the design, the quilt block, should come first, and that it will suggest an overall setting. The parallel in gardening is the person who wants to grow a certain type of flower, say orchids. That flower dictates all further decisions. This is a valid way to work, particularly if you are designing your own quilt block from a live, growing flower. You can't really see the overall quilt until you know how the flower will work in fabric.

Here are two examples of original, unique, flower designs which were certainly inspired by the basic block. Ann Maria Warner (*Figure 2*) apparently had a collection of printed flowers which she had cut from various pieces of chintz or calico. By appliquéing them onto background squares, she devised a way of displaying them, along with some scenic cut-outs of a cottage and some people on a donkey. Within the 57 blocks, not counting the corner stars, there is great variety among the flowers. They are obviously cut from more

than one piece of fabric. Ms. Warner also varied the grouping of people around the donkey — she would cut different people out of the scene, probably to suggest a wider range of action. But the really outstanding feature of this quilt is the Triple Irish Chain sashing which she chose to pull her blocks together. The strong geometry of this pieced sashing not only suggests a fence; it provides weight to the composition. It creates a stable framework in which to mount so many different "pictures." The quilt has no border; as a finishing detail, the four corners are set with blocks in an eight-pointed star design. This quilt represents a skillful solution to the problem of incorporating many different design motifs into a unified whole. The maker appears to have enjoyed appliqué and patchwork more than quilting.

The second example *(Figure 3)* shows the work of a woman who clearly preferred the technique of quilting to piecing or appliqué. It is as though the Delectable Mountains and the Sawtooth borders are there only to add a dash of color. Amazing varieties of floral motifs are worked into the white areas of the quilt. One

Figure 2. Quilt by Ann Maria Warner, 1822; signed and dated, AMW, 1822. Size, 103″ x 105½″.
(Courtesy of The New York Historical Society, New York City.)

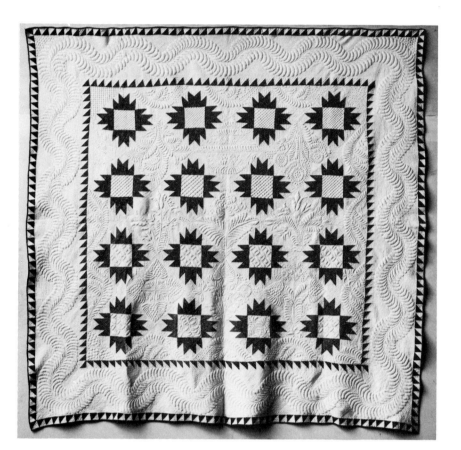

Figure 3. Union Square Quilt by Mary Lawson Ruth McCrea; Indiana; cotton fabrics; signed and dated M.L.Mc., May 18th, 1866. Size, 88″ x 88″. (Courtesy of The Smithsonian Institution.)

of the most prominent of these motifs is the fern frond seen around the outer edges of the center of the quilt. It is reinforced by the feathered cable of the outer border, which looks like a never-ending fern frond. Other botanical motifs include: sunflowers, thistles, berries, tulips, roses, and daisies, as well as an abundance of leaf shapes. This quilt is an example of a technique dictating the design of the overall piece. This was done by a woman who loved to quilt. The beauty of this work is breath-taking. Notice that the very outer corners of the quilt between the feathered cable and the Sawtooth border are quilted! She also had quite an eye for flowers, as the ones she shows are quite realistic in appearance.

It's easy to see that we can approach this business of designing our flower quilt from several angles: function first, as in the quilt with the attached ruffle; aesthetics first, as in the piece with chintz cutouts and the Irish Chain sashing; or technique first, as in the Union Square piece. Of course, successful quilts reflect a careful balance of function, aesthetics, and technique. Each of these three examples achieves that balance, illustrating that any one of the three approaches makes a valid beginning for a quilt design. Any one of them can provide that necessary seed of inspiration.

Now we get down to the work of drawing a quilt design from a live flower. A seemingly impossible task to some of you, but as with any difficult problem, this one is made easier when it is broken down into a series of smaller steps.

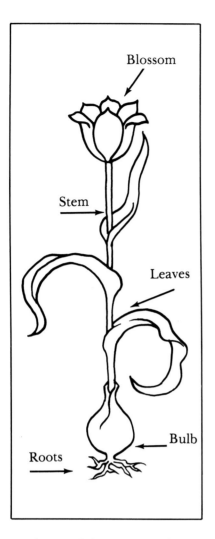

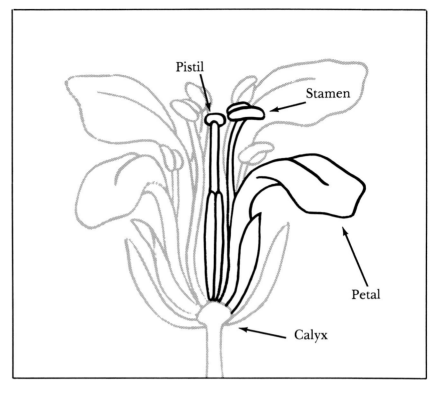

Figure 4. The primary parts of a flower must be identified before designing can begin.

Figure 5 (above). The blossom contains a pistil and several stamens, and one or several rows of petals, the base of which is enclosed by a calyx.

First and foremost, take a good look at your flower and decide what it is you want to feature most prominently. Although it is a joy to look at a plant as a botanist discovering the secrets of plant life, you must also look as an artist, finding beauty in line, form and color. And above all, you must study the flower as a designer, searching for the simple, telling details which can be transformed into a quilt design.

A flower is made up of four primary parts: the roots or bulb, the leaves, the stem, and the blossom *(Figure 4)*. The parts of the blossom vary from flower to flower, depending on how that flower produces pollen—a flower exists solely to reproduce itself in Nature's eyes. Generally, the center of the blossom contains the pistil (the female part) and the stamens (the male part). The stamens produce the pollen, which is often contained in anthers, large seed-looking devices borne at the tip end of the stamens *(Figure 5)*. In some flowers,

such as lilies, the pistil, stamens, and anthers are very prominent parts of the flower, and you could not do a good representation of the flower without them *(Figure 6)*.

The different rows of petals that surround the stamens and pistils perform different functions in the reproduction of the flower, but the main thing that we as designers are interested in is the large, colorful, showy row which attracts insects and forms a landing base for bees (in addition to protecting the pollen and nectar). In most flowers, it is this large showy row of petals that gives the flower its color and dominant shape. However, sometimes there are several rows of petals which may be different colors and shapes. Some marigolds, for example, have several different color petals surrounding a center *(Figure 7)*. In other flowers, such as the petunia and honeysuckle, it is really the second row of petals, known as the corolla, that forms the tube-like shape which appears to be the petals.

Figure 6. A lily design should include a pistil and stamens for a naturalistic representation.

Figure 7 (above). Sometimes each row of petals is different, as in this marigold example.

The very outside row of petals is known as the calyx, and it is made up of individual sepals. Sepals are actually specialized leaves which protect the developing flower bud. They vary in size, shape, and number from flower to flower. In many of our rose designs, the calyx plays a very important part in the design of the bud. Look, for example, at the two rose blocks featured here. In the Ohio Rose *(Figure 8)*, the calyx gains importance because it provides almost all the green in the design, and in the Rose of Sharon *(Figure 9)*, the calyx indicates three buds, varying in maturity.

Figure 8 (above). The buds of Ohio Rose are beginning to peep out of prominent calyxes.

Figure 9 (left). The use of the calyx in this Rose of Sharon design indicates buds in varying degrees of maturity with the largest calyx indicating nearly-open blossoms.

21

But I Can't Draw!

The cry rises immediately to the lips of the novice designer. But, never mind, we can get around that. It's all in the way you look at the flower.

If you are working from a live specimen, study it carefully to determine the most interesting features. You cannot tell everything about a flower in a drawing or in a quilt design, so choose to tell a few things as well as you can. A good pencil outline drawing will be the most practical way to record the details you have selected. It lends itself to a quilt design much more easily than does a naturalistic representation with lots of shading and detailing.

An approach to follow:
1. Study the lines of growth, and indicate them with long, swinging pencil strokes.
2. Sketch in the shapes.
3. Finish with a clear-cut outline.
4. Color in accents as suggested by shadows or dark colors in the plant.

The Camera as a Tool

When natural specimens are not available, photographs of flowers can be used to good advantage. Many fine photos taken by professional photographers are found in books, magazines, and seed catalogs. The only disadvantage to these may be their small size. You may prefer to photograph your own live specimen and work from that photograph. There are two advantages to this; namely, a photo will give you a permanent record of the flower at its freshest, and the camera reduces the three-dimensional object to a one-dimensional plane. It makes it flat and therefore easier to copy. A flower chosen to be photographed should not be so complex that the camera cannot capture it. The photograph should be straightforward, without too many shadows and highlights. Be aware that some photographs and some plants are just not suitable.

Use your photograph to make a flower map. Lay a piece of tracing paper over the photograph and trace the outstanding shapes. You will come up with a rather mosaic-looking tracing, but it has many possibilities. It shows every important part of the flower in outline (*Figure 10*).

Study the flower map to see which shapes you want to feature in your design. Some shapes will suggest appliqué or patchwork; other shapes may suggest a quilting design. Use another piece of tracing paper over the flower map to pull out those shapes you want to work with further.

Let's go back to our original inspiration for a moment. Remember those hollyhocks you had in your mind's eye? First, see if you can't find a nice, growing stand of them to both sketch and photograph. As you study them, you will certainly come to realize that the most outstanding thing about hollyhocks is their height. So back up enough with your camera to get the entire length of the flower stalk in your photograph. Then come in and take close-ups of the beautiful, carnation-type flowers on the stalk. You will refer to your close-up when you plan the individual blossoms and buds, and you will also study it when you start placing your blossoms on the stalk. Take note of all kinds of details when you have the live specimen in front of you; you never know what questions you will have later. Take a photograph of the foliage, the back of the stalk, the calyx, and the inside of the little powderpuff blossoms.

Assuming that you can't find a live, growing stand of hollyhocks, the next best thing to do is to search your seed catalogs, monthly magazines, and garden books for several photos—you will learn something different from each. One may give you the close-up look; the other may give you an indication of the height. You would not fully understand your subject if you saw only one photo.

Figure 10. Make a flower map by placing tracing paper over a photograph and outlining the most important shapes.

As soon as you have your photographs in hand, and the larger the photo the better, you can make your flower map. Make one of both the overall and the close-up. Study each flower map and you will begin to formulate preferences about the flower—what you like best about it. Start transferring those preferences onto a clean sheet of tracing paper. And remember, when making up your own design, *make it to suit yourself.* You have to trust your own choices. If you like the way the hollyhock stands tall but you also like the blossoms, don't be afraid to put slightly oversize blossoms on a tall stem. You don't have to make it look like the real thing; you can make all kinds of wonderful hybrids in your imagination!

When you are satisfied with your basic flower unit, when you have traced and sketched and thrown away and traced and sketched some more, let it rest for a little while. Even a day or two away from the design will give you a fresh perspective. It will also give you a chance to mull over the following questions. How am I going to group the flowers in a basic block? Am I going to use sashing? What techniques am I going to use to construct this design? It was a wise man who said, "It seems that in artistic work, all the faculties of a person must be in play at the same time!"(1)

(1) Richard G. Hatton, *Handbook of Plant and Floral Ornament;* Dover Publications: New York, p. 14.

Figure 11

Figure 12

Figure 13

Figure 14

Figures 11 to 14. Sometimes a botanical finish is the best. Each of these examples shows a simple leaf or bulb at the terminus of the design. Of particular interest is *Figure 11* which shows Carolina Lily worked with Peony, giving us a grand opportunity to study the differences in the two designs. Carolina Lily shows four petals while Peony shows six.

Flower Arranging

As a florist studies the blossoms before she begins an arrangement, so you should study the blossom you've drawn before you begin your arrangement. Pick a proper container, decide on the flowers and greenery you're going to use, and establish your dominant design. Study the different arrangements of Carolina Lily *(Figures 11-19)* for a quick lesson in the amazing variety of designs produced from one basic flower shape.

Study the quilts in "Step Into the Garden" to gain insight into your own decisions about your final design. Do you want a single flower? Two in a vase? Three in a vase? It is generally agreed that groupings of uneven numbers work better than groupings of even numbers.

Study our black and white drawings of individual blocks. Look at the leaves, foliage, and stems of the quilt blocks in this book for inspiration. You may want to take the leaf from one flower and put it on another. Mixing and matching is permitted!

Let's go back to your hollyhocks again. Suppose you said to yourself, "I like them best the way I first saw them, standing straight against a picket fence. That's what I want to try to represent in my quilt design." Having made this decision, you can count on having a long, skinny arrangement of the basic flower, and you can bet that your sashing is going to have to play an important part in representing the fence. You can guess that the open space between the pickets is going to have to be

Figure 15

Figure 16

Figure 17

Figures 15 to 17. Three different containers provide the base for the blossoms of Carolina Lily. In *Figure 15,* three stalks are gathered in a low bowl. The striped sashing used in combination with the checkered red and white corner blocks is particularly interesting. *Figure 16* shows a slightly different bowl or vase. The rather bizarre influence of Art Deco in *Figure 17* makes for a completely unique interpretation of this old pattern. Notice how the bowls are changed into urns by adding handles.

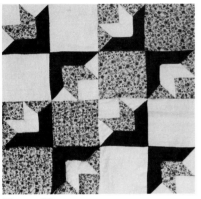

Figure 18

Figure 19

Figures 18 and 19 illustrate arrangements for individual Carolina Lily blossoms other than the traditional three-blossom unit. *Figure 18* is a contemporary execution, while *Figure 19* is a traditional arrangement known as Dove at the Window.

Figure 20. This Hollyhocks quilt, made by Martha Skelton, was a finalist in the 1983 Stearns and Foster Mountain Mist contest. It is now in the permanent Mountain Mist collection.

indicated by the way you handle your negative spaces. As we said earlier, you have to work all your faculties at the same time.

You have established the basic building block of the hollyhock quilt, and you have the other "givens." You can now work out the final plan for the quilt. It may take several tries, but you will eventually devise a plan that suits you. Transfer this plan to graph paper to better understand how the individual components will balance one another. The next step is to make your individual pattern pieces.

A designer for Stearns and Foster gives a possible solution to this design problem in *Figure 20.* The hollyhocks are appliquéd on the sashing which represents the pickets of a fence, and the blocks are empty of pattern except quilting! A unique approach and a perfectly delightful quilt to boot!

Figure 20

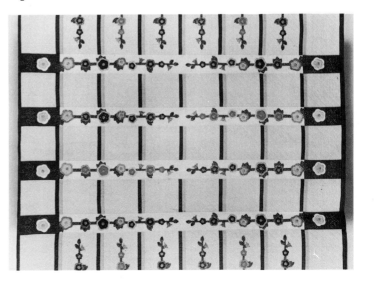

Taking From Established Stock

The oldest camellia in the United States grows in the Middleton gardens, just outside Charleston, South Carolina. It was brought to Middleton Plantation from the Orient during the time the South was actively engaged in trade with China. There's no telling how many camellias, now of venerable age themselves, were taken from this one tree. Just as we take cuttings from established nursery stock, we can and should take quilt patterns from old favorites, especially those in danger of disappearing forever.

I remember being fascinated as a child when I heard one of the women in my mother's quilt group say, "I'm going to take a pattern off that old quilt before I wash it one more time and lose the whole thing." "What?" I thought to myself. "The pattern comes first — how do you go back to the pattern from the stitched quilt?" Because there are many times when an old quilt is beyond restoration, and you can't stand losing the design, we are going to show you how to "go back to the pattern." This will not only help you keep a record of the quilt, but it will give you a tracing from which you can make a new pattern. The technique is also useful for preparing a patch to mend an old quilt.

1. Working on a flat surface, lay out one complete motif of the quilt. Although any hard, flat surface may be used, it is very helpful to have a folding, cardboard cutting board marked off in 1″ squares. The cutting board enables you to use punch pins to hold the tracing paper to the quilt. As an alternative, the tracing paper may be held in place with weights. Buy tracing paper at your art supply store in large sheets to avoid having to tape sheets together.

2. Trace around the entire motif. We used a felt-tip pen which required only the lightest pressure rather than a pencil which could pierce the tracing paper and mark the quilt. Lay a metal ruler along the straight seam lines of the block and trace them. You have now traced the motif "as is." This tracing should only be used to make patterns for replacing or repairing pieces in a quilt.

3. Lay the tracing on a big piece of graph paper. Align at least one straight edge of the motif with a straight line on the graph paper. Mark the center of the design at the top and bottom. The design must now be "trued up," or made square.

Cover the motif with a fresh sheet of tracing paper and trace the outline of the block, squaring it up by following the guidelines on the graph paper.

4. This design is supposed to be exactly the same on both sides of the center. Not only that, both halves of each flower must be identical. To accomplish this, trace one half of one flower onto the fresh tracing paper.

5. Mark the center of the individual flower with tiny arrows. Fold along this line and trace the second half of this flower using the first half as your tracing pattern. Open the fold and you will have a perfectly formed flower.

6. Place the paper back over the original and trace half of the center flower. Mark the center of the flower with tiny arrows.

7. Fold the tracing in half on the center line, or arrows, so the area already copied is visible. Trace all lines from the first half of the design including the first flower. Unfold only when all lines have been traced, and you will have a complete design which is true on both sides of the center line.

8. It is educational to compare your corrected tracing with the original tracing. In our example, it seemed that one corner was more "out of square" than any other area of the drawing.

9. Even more interesting is the comparison of the corrected drawing to the quilt. It is not unusual to find many areas where the corrected tracing and the original do not match, a reminder that fabric will shift and change shape through years of wear and variations in climatic conditions. That is why you must begin a new quilt with a "trued" pattern and patch an old one with untrue pieces. If the quilt doesn't start out as square as possible, there's no imagining the shape it would be in after years of use!

Step 1

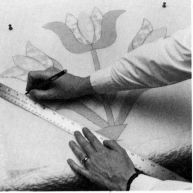

Step 2

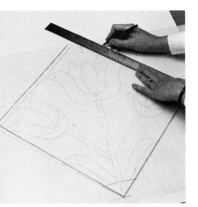

Step 3

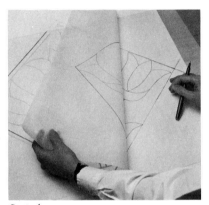

Step 4

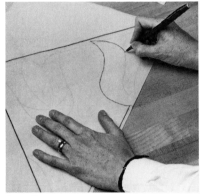

Step 5

Step 6

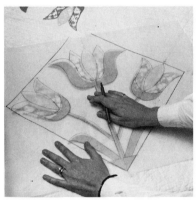

Step 7

Step 8

Step 9

10. As a final step, make note of the fabrics used in the original quilt. You can even trace the print of the calicoes and chintzes if you want a truly accurate record of the quilt. Make note, too, of the quilting (see following page), which, in this case, is ½" squares. Make notes about the backing and binding, and if the borders and sashing are an elaborate pattern, trace a portion of them as well.

Step 10

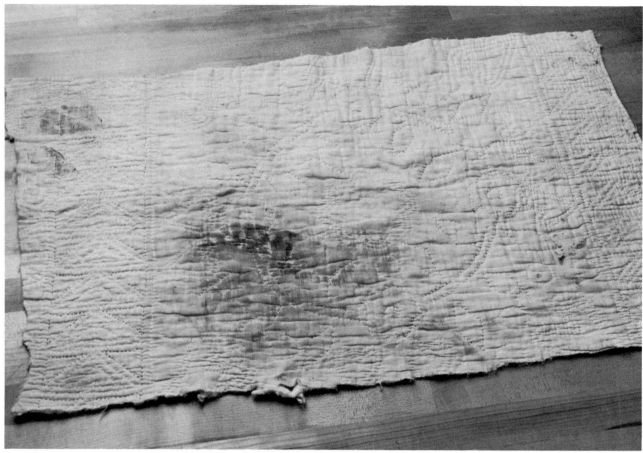

Step 1

It's sad to think a portion of our quilt heritage is lost every year through neglect. Take for example this fragment of what had been a wonderful quilt. When first "discovered" it was being used as an ironing board cover.
1. The print of the iron is clearly visible in several places on the back side of this quilt fragment. The complexity of the stitches tipped off a smart observer that this was no ordinary commercial ironing board cover!
2. A look at the front of the quilt reveals a charming Rose Wreath design with Flying Geese borders and sashing. The background of the square has disintegrated to the point of almost disappearing entirely, but the quilting stitches are still visible. It looks as though the quilting design was even more charming than the appliqué and patchwork!
3. A large piece of tracing paper is placed over the remnant, and the outline of the appliqué wreath is traced, primarily as a guide for positioning the quilting motifs. A pencil with a

Step 2

very soft lead is used for this tracing because it will pick up the "feel" of the silhouettes beneath the tracing paper. The quilt motifs are not visible through the tracing paper, so their outlines must be traced by alternately "feeling" the shape from the top of the tracing paper and lifting up the paper to look for the stitches.

4. Because of the constant lifting of the tracing paper, it is not practical to use push pins or straight pins. We found a glass frog used for flower arranging was heavy enough to keep the corner of the paper in place, but small enough to be out of the way of the tracing.
5. The tracing shows a delightful quilting design of hearts, one in each corner, and two at each rose. A large rose shape is quilted into the center of the wreath. Notes on the tracing indicate how many rows of stitching there are with each motif.

This is the preferred method of lifting a quilt motif from any quilt, no matter what the quilt's condition. First you must establish a point of reference to which you can relate the quilt stitches. The quilting is very often impossible to see through the tracing paper, and this "peep and draw" method must be employed.

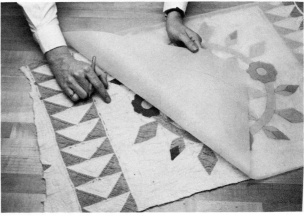

Step 3

Step 4

Step 5

Step Into the Garden

"There is always room for beauty: memory
A myriad lovely blooms may enclose,
But, what soe'er has been, there still must be
Room for another rose."

Florence Earl Coates

The fledgling gardener learns more from a short stroll through an established garden than from hours of solitary study of plant books . . . the experience of seeing the live, growing plant in its natural setting makes a lasting impression. For example, some features of the plant, such as the height and diameter, can be fully appreciated only when one sees it alive and growing. The surrounding environment can also be studied. What other flowers are near? What is the ground cover? Is there a border? Is the bed edged with stone or brick? The great gardens of the world draw thousands of visitors each year simply because they answer questions such as these.

Fabric gardens, cultivated with needle and thread, offer aesthetic experiences similar to the gardens the horticulturalist has planted. We can study the varieties of flowers chosen for stitching — which ones work best in patchwork, which in appliqué? How big is each blossom? How often is it repeated in a grouping? Are the blossoms packed loosely together, or are they set apart in little blocks? Are there formal borders, or does the garden grow over the edges of the quilt? What colors are put together, and what are the background colors? In other words, how does this garden grow?

Our own garden of quilts, in which we now invite you to stroll, presents a selection of some of the many varieties of flower quilts in existence. Just as it is impossible to have one of every flower in your garden, it is impossible to have every flower quilt within the pages of a single book! Some flowers are so popular that one example just won't do — nobody has a rose garden with just one kind of rose in it! The more you look at some flowers, the more you discover about them, and the more variations they seem to take. So you will find several tulips, many roses, an assortment of sunflowers—very much like your garden outside!

Our garden of quilts changes with the seasons, just as Nature directs her own garden to do. The fresh, fragile flowers of early spring give way to the bright medley of summer . . . to the wonderfully fragrant roses which delight us until early fall. A palette of gold and russet greets the fall, with gentle touches of blue and lavender. Winter's flowers are specially treated hothouse varieties, or spectacular specimens preserved from earlier seasons. The nicest thing, though, about a garden of quilts, is that a summer flower is great on a winter bed! While Nature's flowers are gone after a season, a quilter's flowers last through all seasons, year in and year out!

Only one of hundreds of rose designs, our *Ohio Rose* climbs a trellis in Bellingrath Gardens.

30

Prancing, Dancing, Swaying Tulips

*"And 'tis my faith that every flower
Enjoys the air it breathes."*

William Wordsworth

Peachy Tulips *(right)*
An exquisite quilt makes us dream of bridal tables and springtime tea parties. Pattern and description on page 70.

Triple Tulip *(opposite)*
A cascade of pink tulips, blossoming in the quilt and the flower bed. This photograph could tell the story of *A Garden of Quilts* all by itself! Pattern and description on page 66.

Multi-Colored Tulips
Wouldn't you love to have a
bed of fabulous flowers just
like this both outside and inside your home?
Pattern and description on
page 68.

Three Lavender Tulips

And each so different from the others! *Tulips in a Vase*, on the left, is a prim little 1940s arrangement, with a beautiful border. *Heart Tulip*, in the center, has a surprise in the center petal! *Medallion Tulip*, on the right, repeats its basic motif in a most unusual arrangement. All three carry the message of springtime. Patterns and descriptions on pages 74, 64, 72.

From a Southern Garden

*"No occupation is so delightful to me as
the culture of the earth, and no culture
comparable to that of the garden. Though
I am an old man, I am a young gardener."*

Thomas Jefferson

Pink Dogwood
The delight of urban and
rural gardeners alike, the
dogwood is a welcome sight
in early spring.
Pattern and description on
page 76.

Mississippi Springtime
The favorite signs of spring are represented in the center oval of this wonderful, delicate quilt. A cardinal perches gaily among jasmine, dogwood, and magnolia.
Pattern and description on page 78.

Blessings of Spring

"But there's the happiest light can lie on the ground,
Grass sloping under trees
Alive with yellow shine of daffodils!"

Lascelles Abercrombie

Spring Wildflowers *(left)*
A carpet of tiny woodland flowers spreads itself across the forest floor. They know spring is here before anything else does! Find your favorite wildflower and stitch it into a quilt—use wildflower guide books for design inspiration.
Pattern and description on page 82.

Double Daffodils *(opposite)*
These old-fashioned flowers are better known out in the country as "butter and eggs." Bring some inside as soon as they sprout to bloom in your own "conservatory" or plant room.
Pattern and description on page 84.

Dear, Old-Fashioned Posies

"Where are the dear, old-fashioned posies
Quaint in form and bright in hue,
Such as grandma gave her lovers
When she walked the garden through?"

Ethel Lynn Beers

Grandmother's
Flower Garden *(right)*
The bright mosaic in a bed of summer flowers is inspiration for a quilt pattern based on a hexagon. Zinnias and marigolds nod happily over quilts worked in different color schemes and different size hexagons. Pathways, blue on one quilt and green on the others, meander through the flowers in geometric precision.
Pattern and description on page 90.

Johnny Jump-Up
Crawler Quilt *(opposite)*
Fantasy flowers float across this quilt intended just for the youngest member of the family. Are they violas? Primroses? Violets? Pansies? Daisies? You decide!
Pattern and description on page 86.

Peony
This starlike pattern is made up of seven diamonds. What fabulous borders this quilter chose to finish her work of art!
Pattern and description on page 88.

French Nosegay (*opposite*)
An assortment of patchwork posies wrapped in triangles of green march across this beguiling quilt.
Pattern and description on page 92.

Summer Delights

"The summer's flower is to the summer sweet,
Though to itself it only live and die ."
William Shakespeare

Centennial Lily
Nothing says "summer" like a naturalized bed of gold and yellow daylilies. Keep that feeling year-round with this beautiful quilt.
Pattern and description on page 100.

Bird of Paradise
An exotic flower from the jungles of the Amazon provides inspiration for a favorite pattern in a new color scheme.
Pattern and description on page 96.

Bleeding Heart
This most fascinating of flowers produces a bloom within a bloom. The white "heart" opens at its tip to release a red drop of "blood." This equally fascinating quilt captures these unique qualities of the flower.
Pattern and description on page 94.

Dahlia and Basket
A summer quilt on a summer table, laden with the rich harvest of a summer garden. Pattern and description on page 98.

Favorite Flower, Favorite Quilt

"Oh my luve's like a red, red rose,
That's newly sprung in June;
Oh my luve's like the melodie
That's sweetly played in tune."

Robert Burns

Rose Wreath *(left and above)*
Could this be a tribute to the climbing roses that delight us so with their friendly faces and delightful perfume? Pattern and description on page 106.

Tropicana Medallion
(opposite)
Is the rose your favorite flower? Then say so, with the biggest blossom you can stitch!
Pattern and description on page 117.

Whig Rose
The four leaves behind the central blossom, which resemble palm leaves or bristles, are the distinctive characteristic of the Whig Rose pattern. This quilt also bears branches of buds and flowers, some pink, and some yellow.
Pattern and description on page 111.

Rose of Sharon (*left*)
Many quilt patterns are known by this name. This particular variation features 14 buds in each motif!
Pattern and description on page 120.

Victorian Rose (*opposite*)
One simple blossom with greenery is framed by borders of exquisite detailing. A pink Ohio Rose hangs on the quilt rack at the foot of the bed.
Pattern and description on page 108.

Triple Rose

As formal and fancy as the rose garden in which it lies, this quilt features a pink rose with layer upon layer of petals.
Pattern and description on page 114.

Rose and Bird *(right)*

When is too much not enough? This quiltmaker took features from all her rose patterns, and added a bird for good measure!
Pattern and description on page 104.

Ohio Rose *(opposite)*

A classic block arrangement, consisting of a big blossom with four buds, has made this a choice of quilters for over 100 years.
Pattern and description on page 102.

Pretty Climbers

"Flower in the crannied wall,
I pluck you out of the crannies,
I hold you here, root and all, in my hand,
Little Flower—if I could but understand
What you are, root and all, and all in all,
I should know what God and man is."

Alfred, Lord Tennyson

Clematis
Spectacular star-like blooms ensure clematis its place as the best selling climbing plant in the country. Quilt one in bright blue, or look at your favorite seed catalog for other colorations—this flower even comes in stripes! Pattern and description on page 126.

Cherokee Rose *(left)*
This climbing wild rose used to be a familiar sight on the fences and banks throughout the countryside, but urbanization has made it a rare sight. Capture its beauty forever in this quilt.
Pattern and description on page 124.

Morning Glory *(below)*
Get up early to catch the beautiful trumpet-shaped flowers of this little vine. If you spy them before the hot sun does you'll see pink, lavender, and blue, just like in our quilt.
Pattern and description on page 122.

Colonial Favorites

"I have loved flowers that fade,
Within whose magic tents
Rich hues have marriage made
With sweet unmemoried scents."

Robert Bridges

Tulip and Reel
The reel was a favorite geometric shape of the colonists. It has traditionally been adorned with oak leaves and lilies, as well as the tulip shape chosen for this quilt. Notice the cockscomb on the border.
Pattern and description on page 128.

Carolina Lily
Another favorite of our fore-mothers, this design could well be called Colonial Lily. It is worked in one of the most enduring of color schemes—red, green, and white—as fresh-looking today as when it was first conceived!
Pattern and description on page 130.

Pomegranate
This quilt features a motif popular for centuries in crewel work. It has been called a pomegranate in many of its manifestations, but it also represents a bud about to pop into bloom.
Pattern and description on page 132.

Super Sun Lovers

"No, the heart that has truly lov'd never forgets,
But as truly loves on to the close;
As the sunflower turns on her god, when he sets,
The same look which she turn'd on him
when he rose."

Thomas Moore

Triple Sunflower *(right)*
The grandeur of those giants of the garden is captured in a quilt that holds as many sunflowers as is possible!
Pattern and description on page 137.

Marigold *(opposite)*
The name comes from "Mary's Gold," after the Virgin Mary, which is an indication of the esteem in which the marigold is held—it's even been used in a potion to attract sweet dreams, but we don't guarantee fairies!
Pattern and description on page 135.

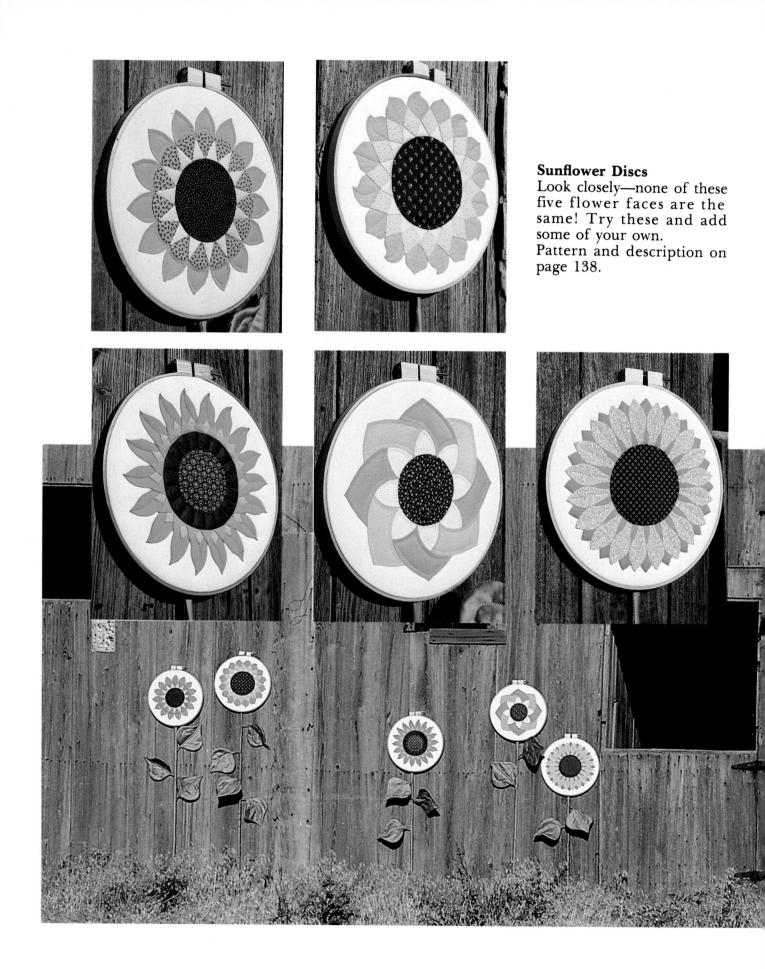

Sunflower Discs
Look closely—none of these five flower faces are the same! Try these and add some of your own.
Pattern and description on page 138.

Colorado Remembrance

When is a quilt block the same as a diary? When it's designed around your favorite memory of a trip! The sunny coneflower is the star of this design.

Pattern and description on page 134.

Winter Flowers

"Announced by all the trumpets of the sky,
Arrives the snow, and, driving o'er the fields,
Seems nowhere to alight: the whited air
Hides hills and woods, the river, and the heaven,
And veils the farmhouse at the garden's end.
The sled and traveler stopped, the courier's feet
Delayed, all friends shut out, the housemates sit
Around the radiant fireplace, enclosed
In a tumultuous privacy of storm."

Ralph Waldo Emerson

Calico Wreath
Winter flowers of white and russet team with stars and flying geese to cheer the table or sideboard all season! Pattern and description on page 142.

Poinsettia

Hothouse poinsettias may brighten your holidays, but this lively quilt will lift your spirits all year long!
Pattern and description on page 144.

Princess Feather

This pattern was originally named after the plume on the Prince of Wales' dress uniform—the Prince's feather. In this example there's a red daisy hiding in the center!
Pattern and description on page 146.

Gardening Tools: The Patterns

"Consider the lilies of the field,
How they grow: they toil not, neither do they spin.
*   But I say to you, that not even Solomon in all his*
glory was arrayed as one of these."

Matthew 6: 28-29

One who works in the earth gathers seed packets and little sprouts, tills the earth, sows her seed, and waits for the flowers to grow. One who works in fabric gathers her pattern, cuts her pieces, and carefully sews each petal in place. Though each works differently, both achieve beautiful gardens. Think of the following chapter as a display of seeds from which you will choose and sew your own flower garden.

We have endeavored to provide full-size patterns for your convenience. The exceptions are few, and are noted on the pattern itself. Very few patterns are given for stems. We suggest you cut them from bias fabric or ready-made bias tape for many of the stems are very curved. Please note that the **pattern pieces do not have seam allowances;** you must add your own. Some quilters like ¼″ seam allowances; others like to use ⅛″. Add the width that suits your own particular style of working.

The number of cuts specified on the pattern piece tells you how many of that shape you need for one block. The shapes or motifs for borders are not numbered because the size of your quilt will indicate how large a border is needed and, therefore, how many times the shape will be repeated.

You may notice that your measurements do not always match those of the original quilt. That is because we have trued up our patterns just as we demonstrated in "Grow Your Own Flower Quilts." The original quilts from which we traced our patterns were sometimes very misshapen, the years of wear and climatic conditions having taken their toll. So just be sure to keep your measurements consistent throughout your own quilt and you'll be fine. Don't worry if it is not exactly the same size as our original. The difference won't be more than an inch or so, in most cases.

Finally, feel free to mix and match leaves and blossoms, or choose different colors, or select a different way of setting the blocks together, and maybe you'll come up with your very own hybrid!

A sunflower pillow made from a fragment of an old quilt duplicates almost exactly the bright blossoms of Mexican Sunflower.
Pattern and description on page 137.

Heart Tulip

(Photograph on page 35.)

Owned by Julia Norman; Old Salem, Alabama.
Made by her mother, Theodosia Smith Norman, and aunt, Belle Gertrude Smith; Fort Deposit, Alabama; 1938.

Measure for Measure *(finished sizes)*

Finished quilt: 84" x 97"

Blocks: 15" square

Sashing: 3" wide, made of three 1"-wide strips, two green and one lavender

Corner blocks in sashing: 3" square (omit on lower outside corners)

Top triangles: 26" x 17⅝" x 17⅝"

Top corner triangles: 19½" x 13½" x 13½"

Side triangles: 25" x 17" x 17"

Bottom triangles: 24" x 17" x 17"

The eye is immediately taken with the vitality of this quilt and its lively, primitive folk art feeling. A second, closer look reveals that the center petal of each tulip is actually an upside-down heart!

The heart is a slightly different color from the outer petals. The leaves and stems are the same green; the sashing and corner blocks are a slightly darker green. The backing is cut from the same lavender fabric as the triangles. In contrast to the off-white muslin background squares, these colors become bright and bold.

Begin appliquéing by first applying the stems and leaves onto a 15½"-square background fabric (allows for ¼" seam allowance). When applying the tulips, appliqué the outer petals in place first, then the heart. Remember, appliquéing curves is made easier when you machine stitch on the fold line and clip to the stitching, then press your seam allowances to the wrong side. Your cutting template makes a handy pressing guide for this.

To make the sashing, cut strips of fabric 1½" x 15½" (allows for ¼" seam allowances). Cut 42 strips from the lavender fabric and 84 strips from the green. Sew one lavender strip between two green strips to form sashing that is 3½" x 15½". Sew the remaining strips in the same way.

To save time at the machine, you might find it easier to cut 1½"-wide fabric strips as long as possible and piece them together to form one long sashing strip. You could then cut this into 15½" lengths as needed.

As you can see from the photograph, the blocks are set together in diagonal rows of five blocks, four blocks, three blocks, two blocks, and a single block. To form these rows, set 3½" x 15½" sashing strips between each block in the row. Then sew solid-color triangles at the ends of the rows (see photo). One row will be only two triangles with sashing between. Next, sew the dark green 3½"-square blocks between each of the 15½"-long sashing strips to form one long strip. Cut this strip to the desired length as you sew it between each of the diagonal rows of blocks.

After basting the backing, batting and top together, outline quilt the tulips, stems, leaves, urn and stripes in the sashing. The lavender

64

triangles are quilted in a diamond pattern, and some random diamond quilting is done in the open area up around the tulip blossoms.

Finish the quilt with a ½″-wide binding cut from the same green fabric as the leaves.

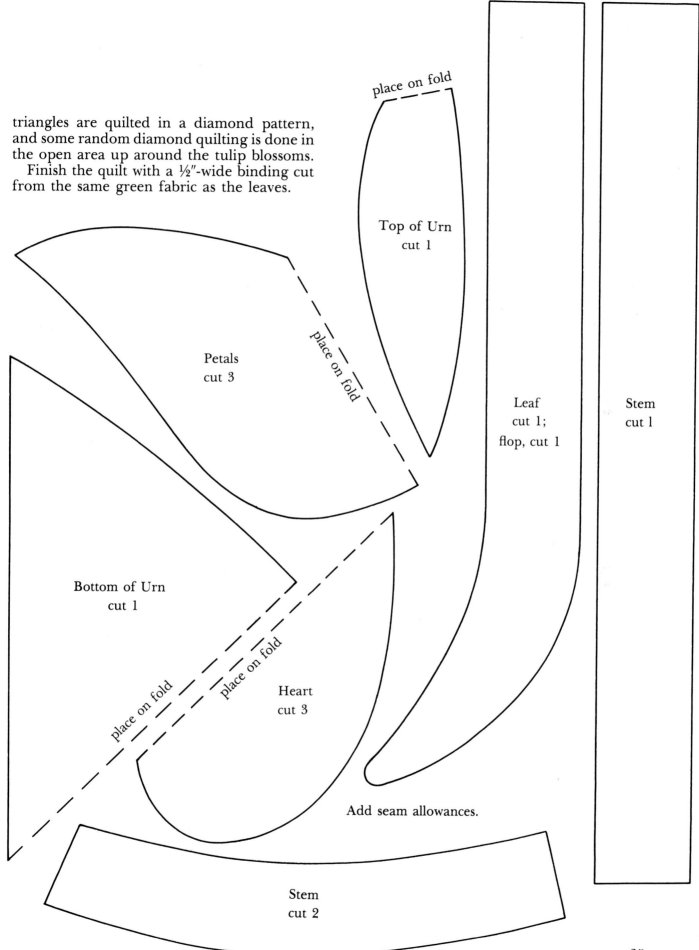

place on fold

Top of Urn
cut 1

Petals
cut 3

place on fold

Leaf
cut 1;
flop, cut 1

Stem
cut 1

Bottom of Urn
cut 1

place on fold

place on fold

Heart
cut 3

Add seam allowances.

Stem
cut 2

65

Triple Tulip

(Photograph on page 32.)

Owned by Imogene Moon Winsett; Hazel Green, Alabama.
Made by her mother, Georgia Della Harris Moon Gilligan; Pond Beat (Redstone Arsenal), Alabama; 1931-1932.

Measure for Measure *(finished sizes)*

Finished quilt: 73″ x 94″

Fabrics: 100% cotton, 45″ wide
   Dark pink: 8 yards (center petals, sashing and backing)
   Light pink: 1¾ yards (outer petals)
   White: 3¼ yards (background of blocks)
   Green: 1½ yards (leaves) and 7½ yards bias tape (stems)

Large tulip blocks: 17″ x 17″

Small tulip blocks in sashing: 4″ x 4″

Sashing: 17″ x 4″

Top borders: 59″ x 7″

Side borders: 91″ x 7″

Binding: ½″ wide

The photograph of this quilt could eloquently tell the story of *A Garden of Quilts* all by itself. The stitched blossoms so realistically capture the life and movement of the real blossoms that you can almost smell that fresh, dewy tulip scent. The grouping of the three tulips and the arrangement of the stems and leaves provide graceful movement and design—one can almost see the gently nodding blossoms in a bed of spring flowers.

The pink, green and white color scheme is a traditional choice for the tulip. The colors in this particular quilt work without being too sentimental because Mrs. Gilligan selected a dark, almost olive green, and made sure that her pinks packed some punch.

To begin your *Triple Tulip* quilt follow the directions on the pattern pieces for cutting tulip petals and leaves. It is important to note the pattern for the side petals and leaves on both the large and small tulips must be flopped, or reversed, to give a right and left side.

The stems of the large tulips are particularly attractive in the way they curve. As all experienced quilters know, achieving a curve like this takes a few "tricks of the trade." Here's what we suggest.

From bias tape, cut 12 stems, each 14½″ long (you will also need 12 straight stems, each 6½″ long). To form the curved portion, run a gathering stitch eight to ten stitches per inch along one long edge of the bias tape. Notice the pressing guide included in the pattern pieces. Trace this guide onto a piece of tracing paper. Glue the tracing onto a square of cardboard, but do not cut out the shape. Pin the bias tape to the cardboard pattern, pulling on the gathering thread to shape the curve along the inner edge of the loop. Using a steam iron, spray the tape with steam and pat it flat, ridding it of any wrinkles or tucks. Allow the tape to dry before removing it from the cardboard and appliquéing it to your background square (see *Centennial Lily* for additional hints on curved stems).

When all appliqué is completed, sew three large appliqué blocks to two vertical rectangles, alternating blocks. This makes one strip. Seam two small appliqué blocks to three alternating horizontal rectangles to complete a second strip. Assemble your entire quilt top by alternately attaching the larger strips to the smaller strips; then attach your borders.

The backing of the quilt is cut from the eight yards of dark pink fabric. Cut one 90″ x 45″ rectangle and two 90″ x 13″ rectangles. Using ¼″ seams, sew one narrow rectangle to each side of the wider rectangle, resulting in a backing piece 90″ x 70½″. Cut your polyester quilt batting 90″ x 70″.

Quilting within the blocks follows the outline of the flower shapes and is spaced in rows about ½″ apart. An interesting triple row of straight stitching quilts the center of the sashing. An additional row ¼″ from the seamed edge completes the quilting here.

When quilting is finished, bind the edges with bias tape or bias strips. This can be made from ten yards of pink bias tape, or you may cut your own bias from additional dark pink yardage.

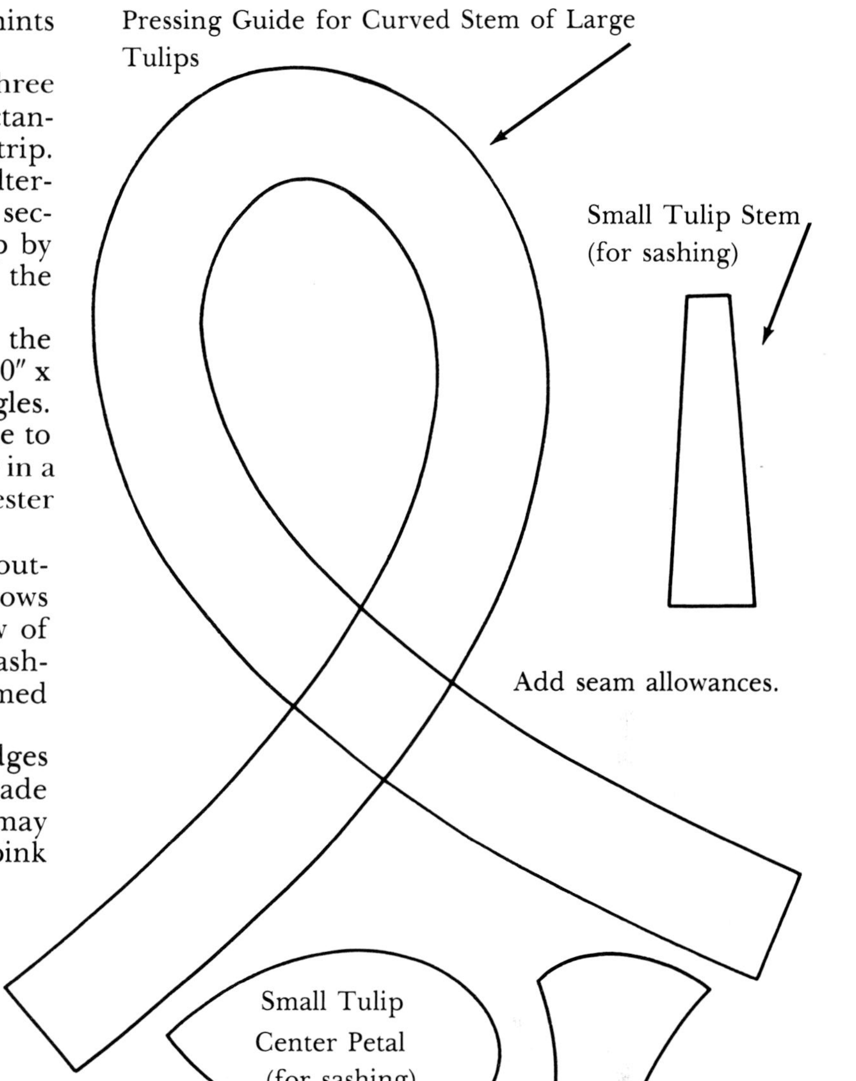

Pressing Guide for Curved Stem of Large Tulips

Small Tulip Stem
(for sashing)

Add seam allowances.

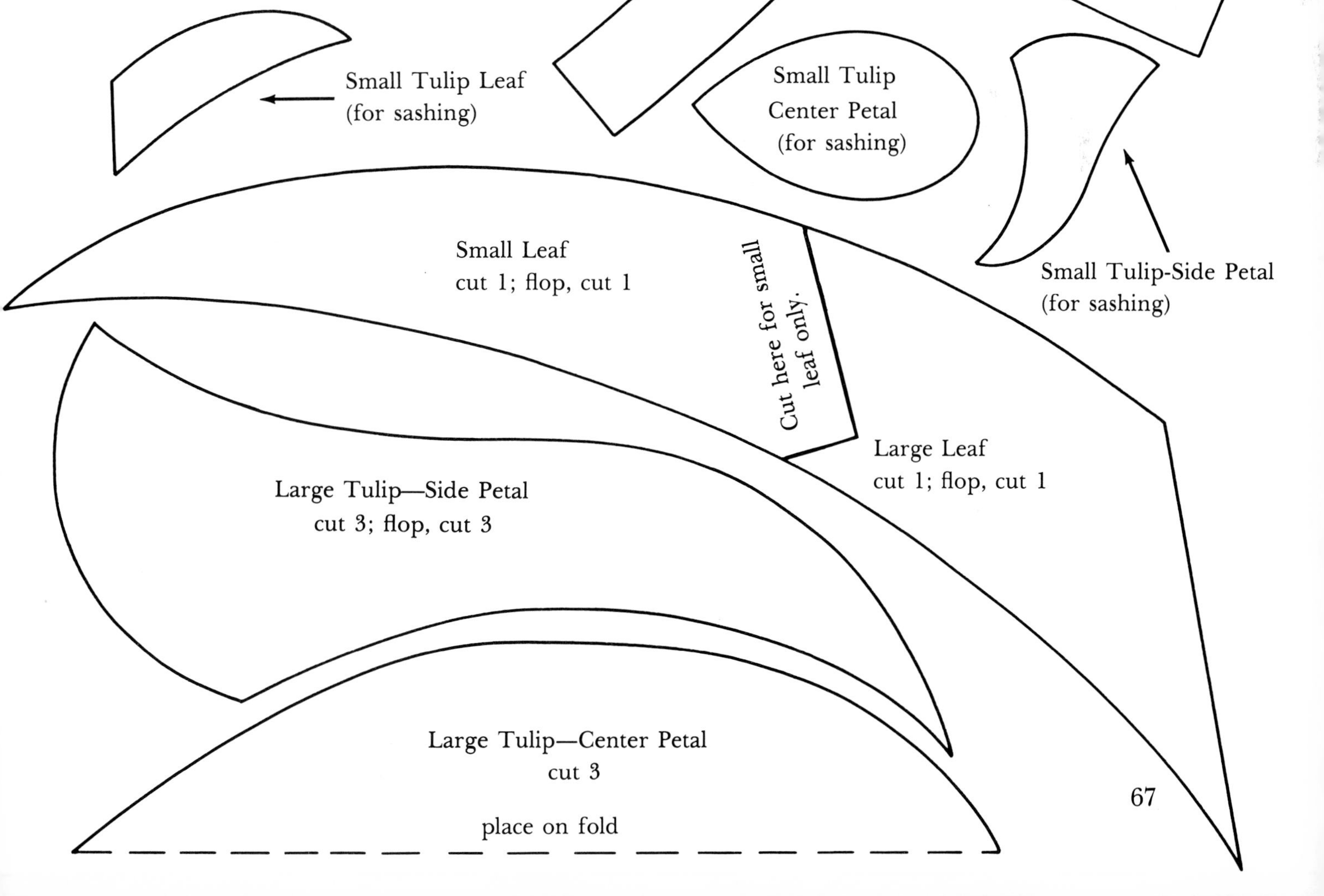

Small Tulip Leaf
(for sashing)

Small Tulip
Center Petal
(for sashing)

Small Tulip-Side Petal
(for sashing)

Small Leaf
cut 1; flop, cut 1

Cut here for small leaf only.

Large Leaf
cut 1; flop, cut 1

Large Tulip—Side Petal
cut 3; flop, cut 3

Large Tulip—Center Petal
cut 3

place on fold

67

Multi-Colored Tulips

(Photograph on page 34.)

Owned by Mary Frances Owensby; Linden, Alabama.
Made by Mary Braznell; Pittsburg, Kansas; 1922.

Measure for Measure *(finished sizes)*
Finished quilt: 70″ x 88½″
Inside center rectangle: 32″ x 50½″
Striped sashing: 3″ wide (each stripe is 1″ wide)
White borders: 16″ wide

The fresh pastels of this color scheme say "Springtime" as eloquently as do the tulips. This quiltmaker decided not to pick one favorite color for her tulips, but used *all* her favorite colors when making this quilt. Pink, lavender, and yellow tulips grow in a neat formal bed in the center of the quilt, and a few windblown flowers are sprinkled around the borders.

The strong colors of the striped inside borders are excellent for defining and supporting the color scheme, which could lose some impact without the help of that inner border. The little checkerboard formed where the stripes cross is a detail that also adds interest to the overall design.

The flowers are appliquéd, the borders are pieced, and the edges are finished with diamond points. Half of these 310 points are dark pink; the other half are light pink. They are alternately placed around the entire outer edge of the quilt (see *Victorian Rose* page 108).

The quilting patterns are feather wreaths and portions of feather wreaths, with the entire background filled with ½″ diamonds. Beautiful stitching forms the patterns and makes this a true masterpiece. It is the quilting that would be a challenge to a beginner; the cutting of the pieces and the appliqué work would not be terribly difficult.

A final note: Mrs. Owensby bought this quilt for $25.00 from her son's Sunday school teacher. The teacher had made it for her only grandson, but decided it was too narrow for his bed. When you measure for your own quilts, remember to take your measurements as if the quilt were "at rest" on the bed. Otherwise, your quilt might be too short or too narrow.

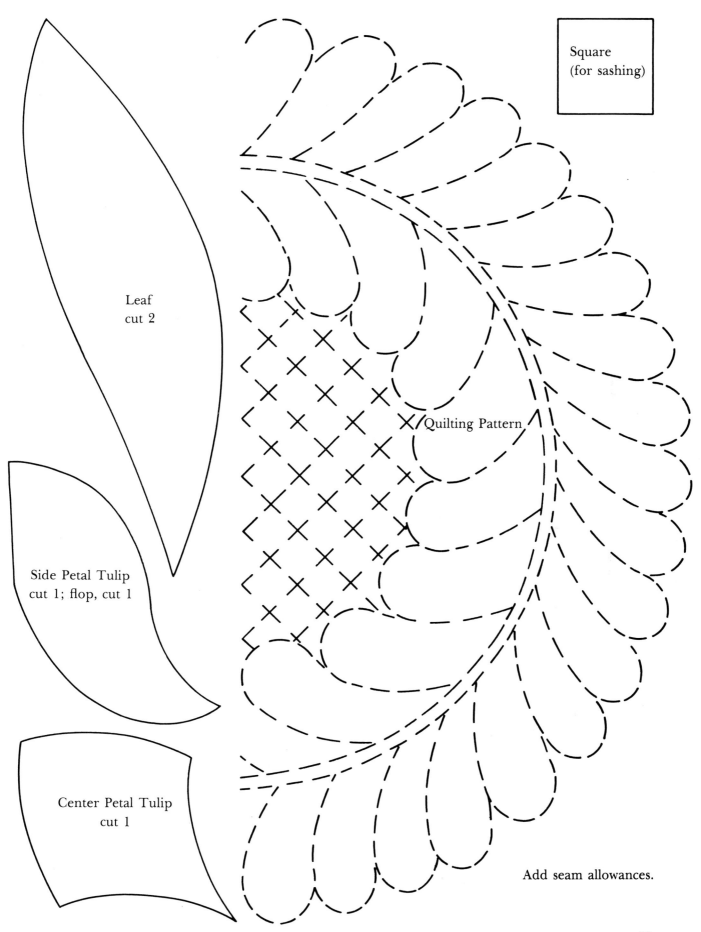

Leaf
cut 2

Side Petal Tulip
cut 1; flop, cut 1

Center Petal Tulip
cut 1

Square
(for sashing)

Quilting Pattern

Add seam allowances.

Peachy Tulips

(Photograph on page 33.)

Designed, made, and owned by Beulah Wilcox Wigley; Robertsdale, Alabama; 1976.

Measure for Measure *(finished sizes)*

Finished quilt: 67¾″ x 67¾″

Blocks: 22½″ square

Inside border (dark peach): 2″ x 49½″

Second border (medium peach): 4″ x 57⅜″

Outside border (light peach): 5″ x 67¾″ ·

Binding (light peach): ⅜″ x 272″ (cut from bias)

Backing (light peach): 67¾″ x 67¾″

Batting: Polyester

A *tour de force* in design is achieved in this work through the use of sensuous, graceful curves framed within a square format. The straight-lined, almost striped borders provide a necessary counterpoint to the curves of the blossoms, stems, leaves and quilting. It is skillful manipulation of the linear design elements that makes all of the components work together successfully.

The four central blocks within the quilt each contain four leaves and three tulips joined by curving stems. After the blocks have been sewn together by machine the curving stems form a secondary central pattern, suggestive of a *fleur-de-lis,* or lily of France. Once this large square is formed, all the borders are attached by machine. Hand stitching is used throughout the remainder of the quilt; this includes mitering the corners.

The simple color scheme is composed of three colors: peach, white and green. The variations on the peach, including a very dark, almost rust color, are well chosen, and the olive green is very close to the natural color of tulip leaves and stems.

The quilting inside the central square is what Beulah Wigley calls Hawaiian quilting. It is similar to outline quilting, except that while the stitching is following a shape, it is also forming a different and distinctive shape of its own. This can be seen in the elongated diamonds between the blossom and leaf. The borders are quilted in a cable pattern, varying

from 1½″ wide to 4″ wide, depending on the width of the border. This twining cable repeats the oval shapes of the curved green stems and the central petal of each flower. Of particular note is the way the quilting is handled at the corners.

This is not a time-consuming project, as quilt projects go. The forming of the curved stems is the most difficult part, but if you cut the stems on the bias and follow Martha Skelton's suggestions (see *Centennial Lily*), you shouldn't have any trouble.

Since Beulah Wigley has taken up rug hooking as enthusiastically as she did quilting, *Peachy Tulips* was her last quilt. What a grand finale!

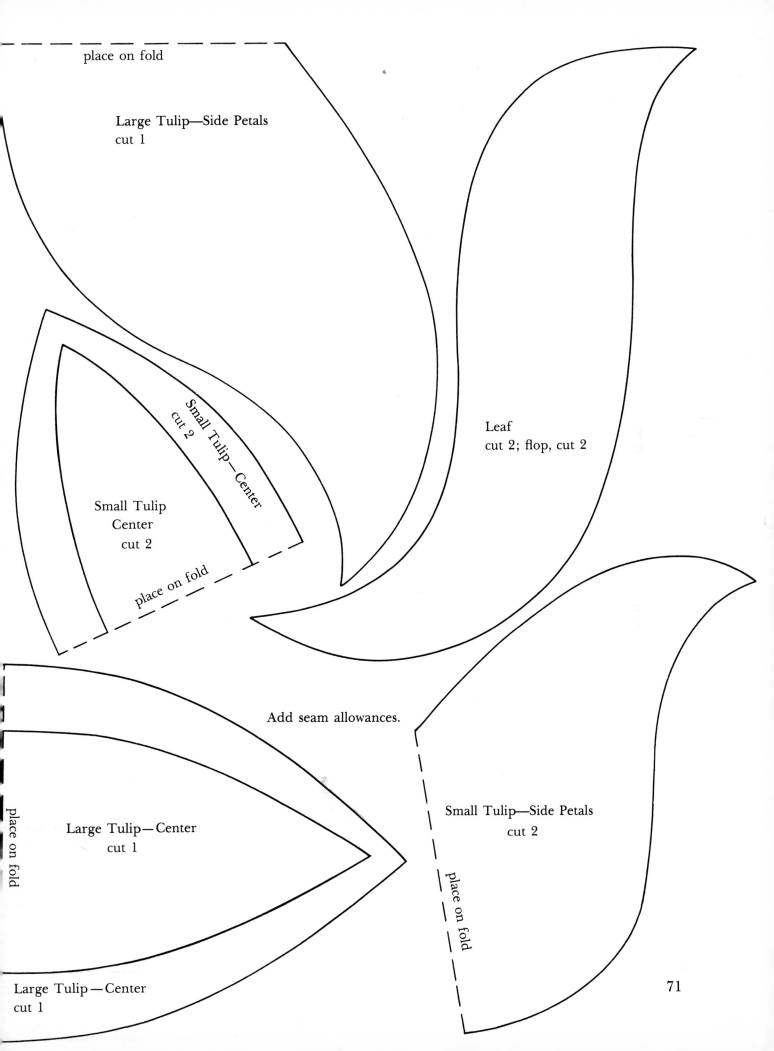

place on fold

Large Tulip—Side Petals
cut 1

Small Tulip—Center
cut 2

Small Tulip
Center
cut 2

Leaf
cut 2; flop, cut 2

place on fold

Add seam allowances.

place on fold

Large Tulip—Center
cut 1

Small Tulip—Side Petals
cut 2

place on fold

Large Tulip—Center
cut 1

71

Medallion Tulip

(Photograph on page 35.)

Owned by Rick and Mary Greenbaum;
Dallas, Texas.
Provenance unknown; 1930.

Measure for Measure *(finished sizes)*

Finished quilt: Approximately 68½" x 80½"
Central block: 21" x 21"
Figured blocks: 10½" x 10½"
Plain blocks: 10½" x 10½"
Half blocks: 10½" x 10½" x 15"
Quarter blocks: 7" x 7" x 10½"
Border: 4" wide
White stripes: 1½" wide
Lavender stripe: 1" wide
Binding: 1" wide

This spritely little tulip quilt owes its impact to an unusual arrangement of the basic block. Four of the blocks make the center medallion; groups of three blocks are gathered at the top and bottom, and the sides are marked with five blocks set side by side. The white field provides plenty of space for intricate quilting. The lavender half-blocks around the edge of the quilt act as a border, almost three-dimensional in that they reach into the tulip blocks. Together, it makes for one of the most interesting and appealing quilts in this collection.

This is the only one of our tulips to employ a print fabric. The print chosen for the center petal perfectly matches the pinky-lavender of the solid. The lavender itself is unique in that it is by far the "warmest" used in our collection of lavender tulips — the others are far more "blue."

Three tulips, each with three petals, are gathered along with two leaves into a green triangle in one corner of each figured block. The 6" and 4" stems of the tulips are a brighter green than the leaves or the corner triangle and appear to have been made from commercially-prepared bias tape. Sixteen of these blocks are worked just alike on 10½" x 10½" squares. For the center medallion, the four squares are cut as one — one 21" x 21" square. The design is worked just like four individual squares, except that a 6" x 6" green square is placed in the exact middle of the quilt at the

junction of the stems, in place of the four green triangles.

The quilting in the solid white blocks might best be described as a modified sunflower. A 7" circle, filled with ¾" diamonds, is ringed by eight petals which grow larger to reach into each corner of the block. Each appliquéd tulip is outline quilted, and the half-blocks and border are stitched with 1" diamonds. The backing and binding are white, and the batting is cotton.

Altogether charming, this little quilt pattern would be a good choice for a beginner's first appliqué flower quilt. Satisfaction is practically guaranteed—who could resist its bright appeal? And the pieces aren't difficult to handle: there are only three pieces per blossom, two leaves, and the corner triangle, making 12 pieces per motif. Use packaged bias tape for the stems, and the blocks will go quickly.

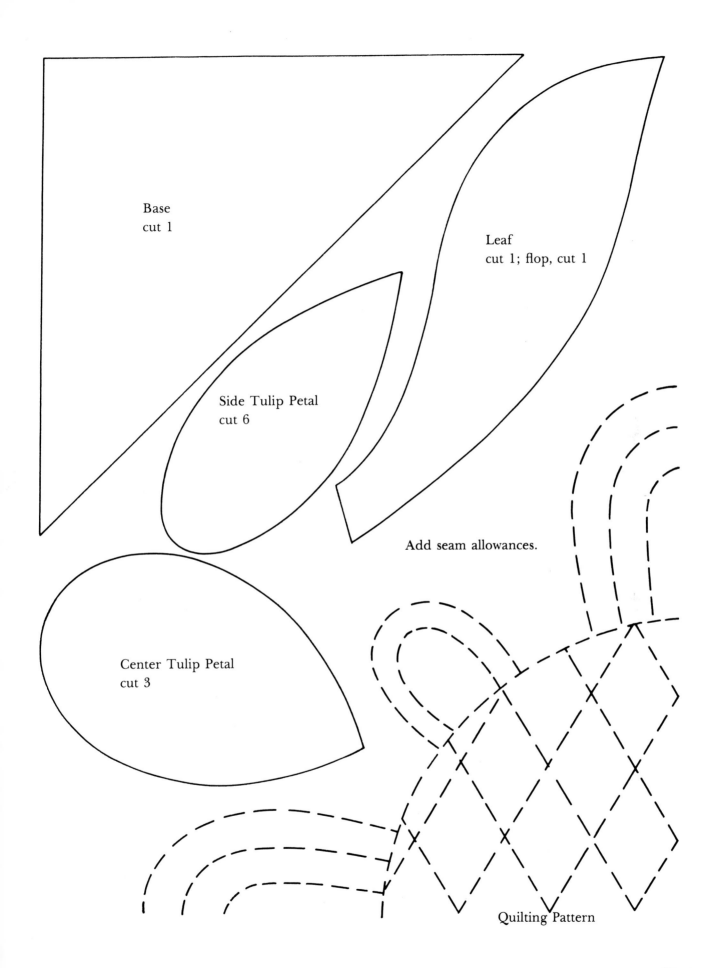

Base
cut 1

Leaf
cut 1; flop, cut 1

Side Tulip Petal
cut 6

Add seam allowances.

Center Tulip Petal
cut 3

Quilting Pattern

Tulips in a Vase

(Photograph on page 35.)

Owned by Rick and Mary Greenbaum;
Dallas, Texas.
Provenance unknown; 1930.

Measure for Measure *(finished sizes)*
Finished quilt: 80¾" x 98½" (53¼" x 71" before borders and binding)
Figured blocks: 12½" x 12½"
Plain blocks: 12½" x 12½"
Half blocks: 12½" x 12½" x 18"
Quarter blocks: 8½" x 8½" x 12½"
Borders: 13½" wide
Batting: Cotton
Binding: ¼" wide

If you were asked to name the colors of early spring, your answer would have to be soft green, white, and lavender. This pastel palette colors the landscape of woodland and garden alike, before the bolder yellows and pinks of later spring appear. Although the flower represented here is the tulip, this quilt makes us think of other spring flowers as well. We are reminded of the violet, the iris, the crocus, even the lilac—all those wonderful purple and lavender flowers that are such a welcome sight to winter-weary eyes.

This is one of the prettiest quilts we've seen. The delicate blending of the greens and lavenders is just right. The graceful arch of the tulip stems is repeated in the curve of the leaves and in the urn or vase in which they grow. The swags and blossoms of the border emphasize a feeling of grace and serenity. The maker of this quilt added her own touch of individuality by making only the side borders pale pink. The background of the rest of the quilt is white. The white of the top and bottom borders meet at a mitered corner in which the swag of the border has also been mitered so it turns the corner perfectly.

The workmanship in this quilt is as good as the design. Each flower, each stem, each leaf is appliquéd with the tiniest of stitches. The quilting of the plain blocks repeats in silhouette the pattern of the figured blocks—so perfectly that it looks as though it were traced.

The tallest tulip blossom and the two short leaves are quilted in the half-blocks, and a single blossom adorns each quarter block. Because every piece of appliqué is outline quilted, border included, the back of the quilt is a perfectly stitched duplicate of the front, except for the colors, for the backing is white.

Although this is not a terribly difficult pattern, it probably should not be a first quilt because there are some curves and points to be mastered. A test block will give you the answer as to the difficulty you will experience. It may go quite easily for you.

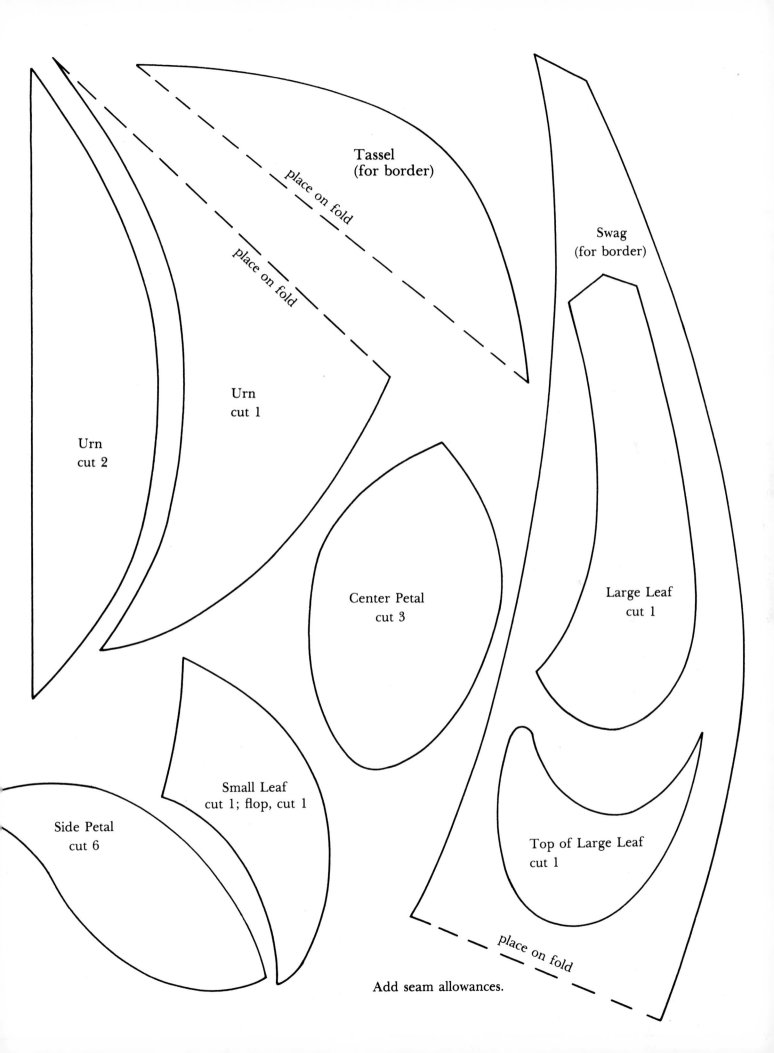

Tassel
(for border)

place on fold

place on fold

Swag
(for border)

Urn
cut 1

Urn
cut 2

Center Petal
cut 3

Large Leaf
cut 1

Small Leaf
cut 1; flop, cut 1

Side Petal
cut 6

Top of Large Leaf
cut 1

place on fold

Add seam allowances.

Pink Dogwood

(Photograph on page 36.)

Designed, made and owned by Helen Whitson Rose; Nauvoo, Alabama; 1979.
Quilted by two sisters, Millie Atkins and Betty Smith; Nauvoo, Alabama.

Measure for Measure *(finished sizes)*

Finished quilt: 101″ x 101″

Fabric: Cotton/polyester blend

Blocks: 12″ x 12″

Border: 2″ wide

Batting: Polyester

Binding: ⅜″ wide, cut from 2″-wide pink bias strips

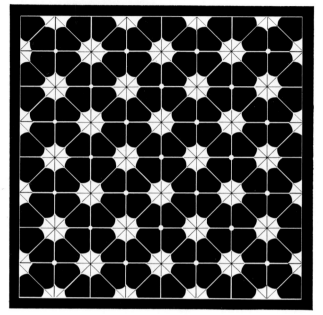

What a wonderfully imaginative way to design a dogwood blossom for patchwork! The haunting beauty of this tree is difficult to capture with fabric and thread, but Mrs. Rose has done just that in this beautiful quilt. The blossoms are spectacular in this size, reminding us immediately of the pleasant shock we have when we spot the dogwood blooming underneath taller trees. The deep avocado green of the quilt hints at the dark, shaded forest floor which provides such a perfect backdrop for the blooms. When the blocks of this quilt are joined, we receive a lagniappe in the form of a secondary pattern. This shape suggests a spider's web — a spider's web glistening with spring dew! Mrs. Rose vows she did not plan the webs; they just appeared when the blocks were set together.

As effective as the color scheme is, it's not the only reason the quilt design is successful. It consists of two petals; one is on a white background, and one is on a green background (see photo). Mrs. Rose was very clever to break down the design to this building block. It's easily managed, it provides a fabulous effect, and it gives very little hint of the overall pattern. Truly, patchwork at its finest!

This is a big quilt, 101″ x 101″, made to fit a king-size bed. If you want a smaller quilt, omit a row of blocks. A quilt of this size requires the following 45″-wide fabric yardages:

Rose or soft pink: 6½ yards
Avocado: 3 yards (includes border)
White: 11 yards (includes backing)
Yellow: ¼ yard

To make a single 12″ block, sew two white corner pieces to a pink petal and two green corner pieces to another pink petal. For ease in stitching, you should first clip the curved edge of the corner piece seam allowance at its deepest point, then pin this to the petal. The curved seam goes together easily when the corner piece is on top of the petal. Hand stitch along the seamline with tiny stitches, then press the seam allowances toward the petal. When both petals have been joined to corners, sew the block together on the long diagonal to form a 12″ square. This last seam and all other joining seams may be done by machine for speed and extra strength.

The flower centers are added after the blocks have all been joined together. Cut the flower centers from yellow fabric, remembering to add a seam allowance. Run a gathering stitch around the circle in the seam allowance. Cut a cardboard pressing guide from the pattern and place it inside the circle. Pull up the gathering thread tightly but do not fasten off. Press the edges around the card-board circle and crease. Remove the card-board and stuff the circle lightly with a bit of fiberfill. Pull the thread up tightly again and fasten off. Pin the padded circles in the center of the flower where four blocks meet, and from underneath the quilt top stitch with tiny running stitches.

The actual quilting of this piece was done by two sisters who, as Mrs. Rose puts it, "have the same stitch." Each petal is outline quilted ½" from the edge; the yellow centers are quilted about ⅛" to the outside, and three straight lines radiate from the center of each petal. Perhaps the most effective quilting of all though is in the secondary designs, where rows of outline quilting approximately 1" apart reinforce the feeling of a spider's web. The borders are quilted along the seams and exactly down the center.

This cheery, exquisitely simple design is relatively easy to execute. Choose a soft pink and the right green, and you will have an heirloom to treasure for years.

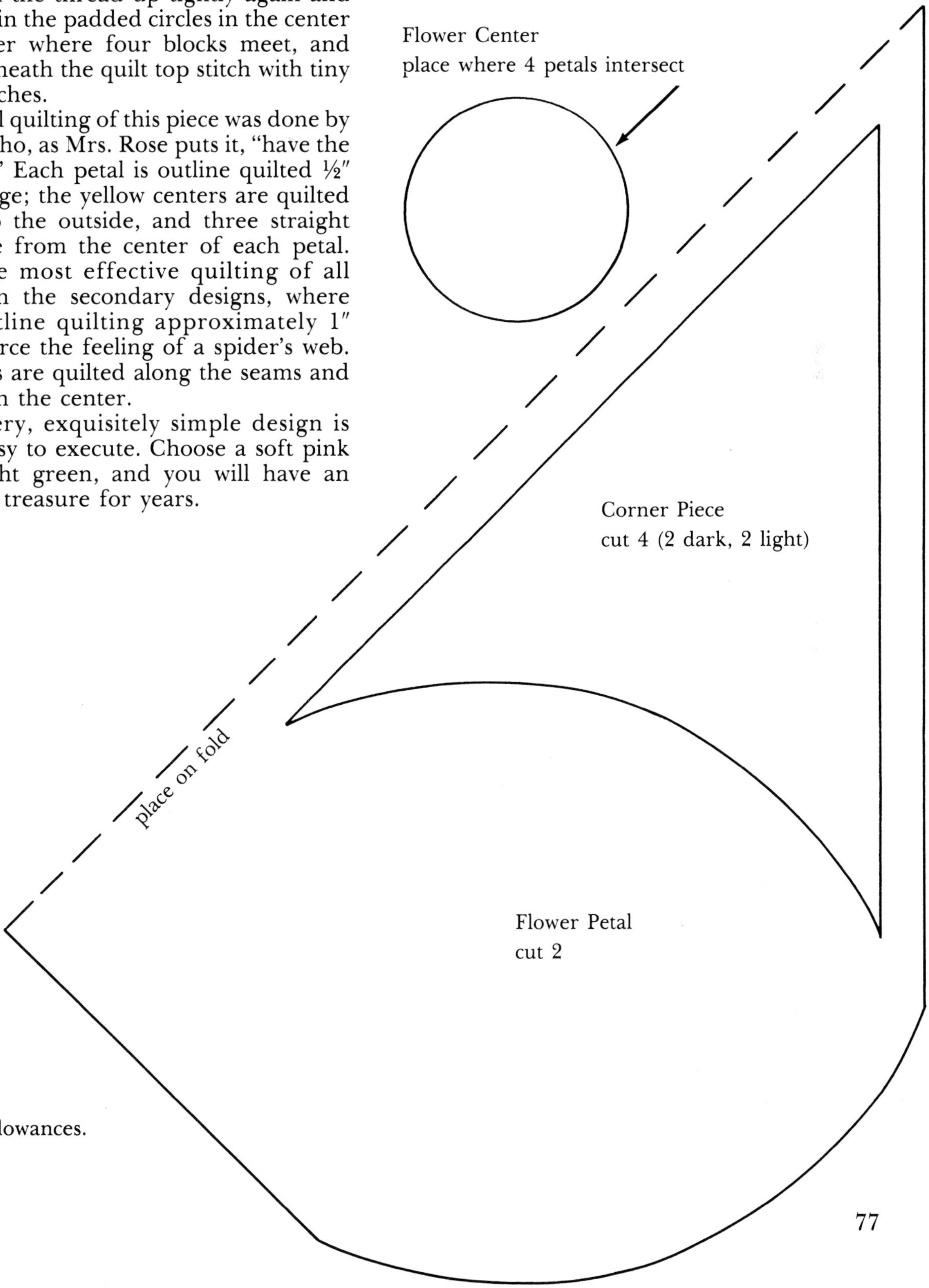

Flower Center
place where 4 petals intersect

Corner Piece
cut 4 (2 dark, 2 light)

place on fold

Flower Petal
cut 2

Add seam allowances.

77

Mississippi Springtime

(Photograph on page 37.)

Designed, made, and owned by Martha Skelton; Vicksburg, Mississippi, 1976.

Measure for Measure *(finished sizes)*
Finished quilt: 76" x 95"
Center oval: Approximately 35" across, 46" long
Center panel: 42" wide with 17" panels added to each side
Backing: Pieced with a center seam

A traditionalist's delight, this lovely quilt combines the favorite harbingers of spring in the Deep South: dogwood, jasmine, magnolia, and cardinal. These motifs are worked into a graceful oval for a center medallion, and the flowers are repeated in a quilted border.

The creamy white color of the magnolia and dogwood is complemented by the beige background. The leaves of the magnolia blossoms are made from three shades of green fabric and a fourth green, brighter than those in the magnolia, is used for the dogwood leaves. The random leaves of the wreath again repeat the magnolia colors. Dark leaves, the same color as the magnolia's, are chosen for the jasmine. A pale beige thimble of fabric forms the center of the magnolias, and an even paler beige makes the outer petal edge. Dark brown fabric is used as the stem for the magnolia and the dogwood, but only stem stitching is fine enough for the stem of the jasmine. Touches of embroidery are used as the center of the trumpet of jasmine (dark yellow straight stitches), at the outer tips of the dogwood petals (dark brown straight stitches), and in the center of the dogwood (yellow-green straight stitches).

The purity and simplicity of this design are enhanced by the way it is quilted. The background of the center section (51" x 62") is quilted with 1¾" squares set on the diagonal to form diamonds. The 15½" borders on the top and bottom and 12" borders on both sides are quilted with the flower silhouettes. The magnolia is centered at the top and placed along the bottom of the quilt's borders. The curved designs on either side of the magnolia are slightly straightened for the quilting design. The birds are omitted and replaced with a dogwood and four leaves that curve up to finish the corner. On the side border, the dogwoods and jasmine sections are repeated three times and the magnolia and cardinal are omitted. To get your pattern for quilting, choose the sections of the oval that you want to quilt and trace around them.

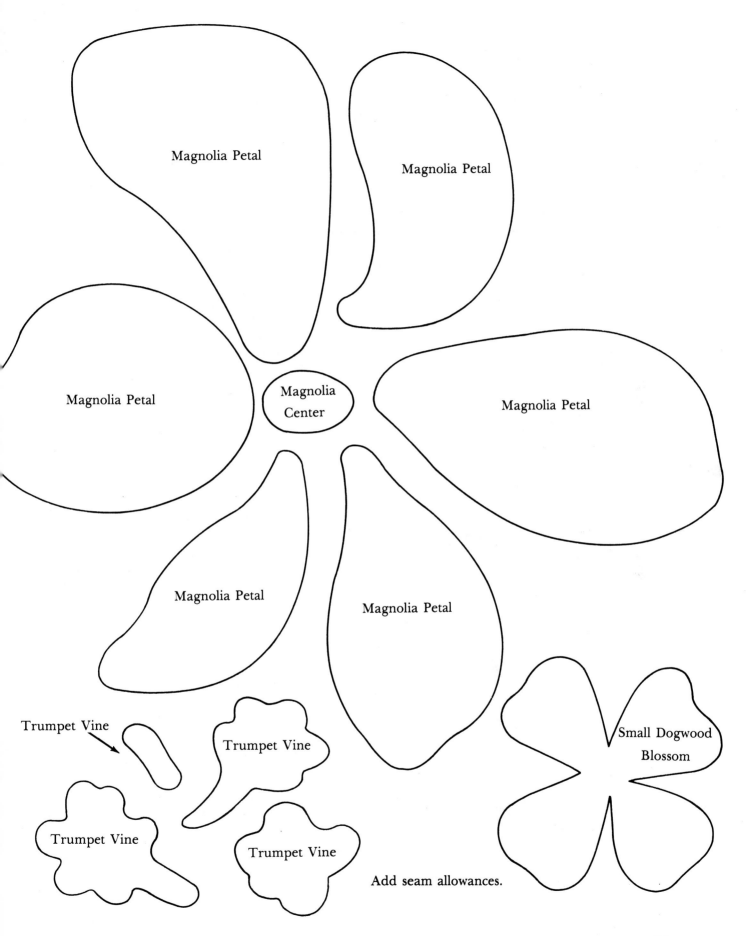

Magnolia Petal

Magnolia Petal

Magnolia Petal

Magnolia Center

Magnolia Petal

Magnolia Petal

Magnolia Petal

Trumpet Vine

Trumpet Vine

Trumpet Vine

Trumpet Vine

Small Dogwood Blossom

Add seam allowances.

Pattern continued on next page.

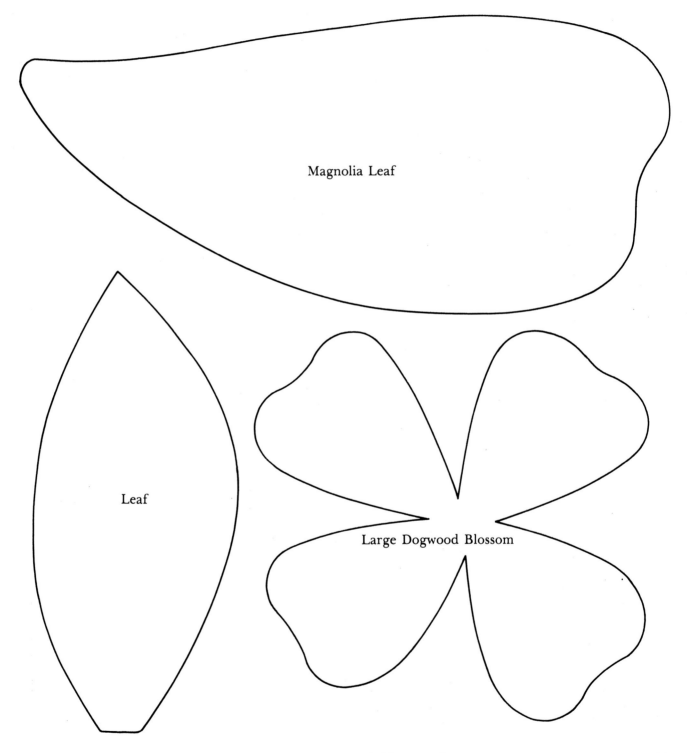

Magnolia Leaf

Leaf

Large Dogwood Blossom

Add seam allowances.

Pattern continued on next page.

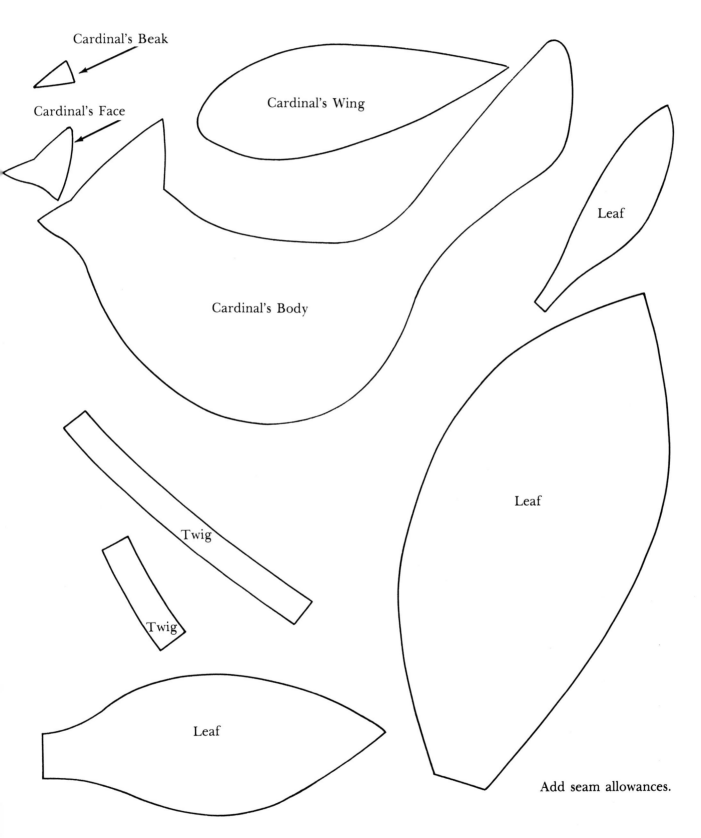

Cardinal's Beak

Cardinal's Face

Cardinal's Wing

Leaf

Cardinal's Body

Leaf

Twig

Twig

Leaf

Add seam allowances.

81

Spring Wildflowers

(Photograph on page 38.)

Owned and quilted by Lois Dukes Booker; Foley, Alabama, 1976.
Pieced by an anonymous person in 1942; date embroidered at top of quilt.

Measure for Measure *(finished sizes)*
Finished quilt: 75" x 89"
Hexagons: 5" x 7¼"
Border: 5½" wide at widest part; quilted to look as if it were pieced with hexagons.

This happy little quilt consists of 179 different fantasy wildflowers, carefully appliquéd onto white broadcloth hexagons. Careful examination reveals no two flowers are alike! There are similarities, but no two are identical. Each flower has a curved stem with one leaf, but even the leaves vary in shape. Some are grassy blades while others resemble a silhouette of a holly leaf. The free-hand shapes of these spring blossoms are reminiscent of tiny wood iris, bluebell, crocus, pansy, columbine, and buttercup.

Piecing this quilt would be a wonderful way to while away time watching television, commuting, or traveling. It looks as though the maker of the quilt laid on her stem and leaf first, and then sewed down the flower of her choosing, probably making up the flower as she went along. One flower even has a tiny six-pointed star for a center! We give you several shapes to get you started, but encourage you to experiment and create your own flowers. Those who fret about piecing being repetitive have certainly found their quilt here!

The hexagons are joined in lengthwise rows: nine rows of eleven blocks, and eight rows of ten blocks. The rows are then sewn together by hand to maintain perfect inside and outside corners.

Mrs. Booker said she nearly wore out the quilt top carrying it around trying to find a border that would complement all the colors in the quilt. When she saw this pink sheet, she knew she'd found just the right thing! The borders are cut from the sheet to fit around the hexagons and are wide enough to allow a 1¼" hem. The backing is white broadcloth.

Mrs. Booker's quilting is minimal, with each hexagon being stitched ¼" inside and outside seams. By quilting the same size hexagons in the border area, she did a wonderful job of integrating the border and the quilt top.

As we encourage you to do, Mrs. Booker has dated and signed the back of the quilt. The front of the quilt had been embroidered with the 1942 date, so the history of the quilt is permanently documented.

By the way, this quilt top, along with a couple of others, was found in an old trunk bought at a flea market. Aren't we all fortunate that it fell into Mrs. Booker's hands!

Hexagon

Center

Flower

Center

Flower

Center

Flower

Leaf

Flower Petals

Center

Stem

Leaf

Stem

Flower

Flower

Flower

Center

Flower Petals

Flower Petals

Center

Add seam allowances.

83

Double Daffodils

(Photograph on page 39.)

Owned by Beulah Wilcox Wigley;
Robertsdale, Alabama.
Pieced by an anonymous person, quilted by
Rubena Elizabeth Ard Wilcox Boyington;
Robertsdale, Alabama; 1958.

Measure for Measure *(finished sizes)*

Finished quilt: Approximately 89½" x 90" or
   67½" x 76" before borders
Figured blocks: 13" x 13½"
Plain blocks: 13" x 13½"
Half blocks: 13½" x 13½" x 21¼"
Quarter blocks: 9½" x 9½" x 13"
Border: 14" at deepest point of scallop

Nothing inspires a winter-weary soul like spring's first daffodil. The only thing better than one daffodil is a field of daffodils. They give us the impression of having escaped the civilization of a formal yard to run off and play in the meadow!

Our daffodil is the double kind, cut out of three different yellows — varying from light butter yellow to deep egg yolk—like the old-fashioned "butter and eggs" found around old houses down South. The center of these flowers is a cluster of light and dark colored petals, and the outer edge of larger petals is a medium bright yellow. The proportion of the bloom to the stem and leaf is appropriate in this design. Who really notices those parts compared to the heavenly blossom? Notice the leaves and stems are each cut from different green-colored fabrics.

Twelve figured blocks are set with six plain white blocks. The white, yellow and green scalloped border is reminiscent of a lady's fancy petticoat and the perfect way to finish out this wonderful quilt. The quilt is greatly enlarged by the addition of the border. These swags are 14" deep at their widest point, but you could make yours wider or narrower. Decide on the width you need before making your pattern. The borders are pieced on the sides. Bias binding is finished to a width of ½".

Batting is a thin cotton sheet, and the backing is white cotton which makes this a perfect summer quilt or spread. Quilting fills the large white blocks with 1" diamonds. Outline stitching follows the flower shapes, and the borders provide the pattern for rows of quilting spaced 1½" apart within each border.

The story of this quilt is quite amazing. Mrs. Boyington was taking the trash out one day while visiting a relative in Los Angeles when she saw this quilt top in the garbage can. She promptly rescued it, washed it, and quilted it, and that's why we can enjoy it today. It's unbelievable that anyone could part with a top this pretty!

Note: If you're looking for a pattern for a single daffodil, check Recommended Reading for sources.

84

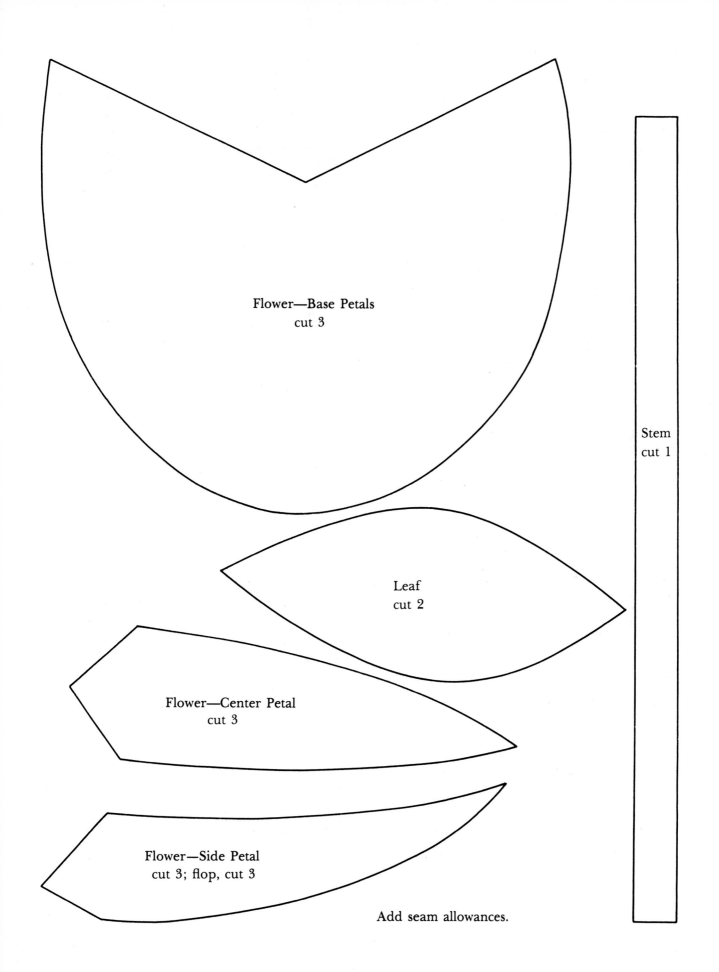

Flower—Base Petals
cut 3

Stem
cut 1

Leaf
cut 2

Flower—Center Petal
cut 3

Flower—Side Petal
cut 3; flop, cut 3

Add seam allowances.

85

Johnny Jump-Up

(Photograph on page 40.)

Designed, made, and owned by Martha Skelton; Vicksburg, Mississippi; 1980.

Measure for Measure *(finished sizes)*
Finished quilt: 58" x 59"
Johnny Jump-Up blocks: 15¼" x 15¼"
Daisy blocks: 15¼" x 15¼"
Sashing: 2" x 15¼"
Corners of sashing at center block: 2" squares
Border: 3¾" wide, 50¾" long
Corner blocks: 3¾" square
Binding: ⅜"

Country folks just love to spread their quilts on the ground and put things on them—their babies, for example! A quilt makes a great playpen for an infant. It's soft and clean and it protects the baby's tender little skin from sharp pine needles and twigs and pesty ants. Some folks say that a crawling baby will stop at the edge of the quilt rather than go off it because he fears there is nothing beyond the edge. We can't vouch for the authenticity of that statement, but we do know that babies and quilts go together!

This is Martha Skelton at work again, and the attention to detail on this little quilt is meticulous. The playful colors and simple shapes remind us of Johnny Jump-Ups, a wonderful little old-fashioned flower we don't see much anymore. The cleverly combined prints in each of the flowers are a happy mixture from the scrap bag. The chartreuse used for the sashing, border, and binding is the perfect accent, especially when played against the dark green and yellow of the randomly placed leaves and stems. The flowers, leaves, and stems are appliquéd onto the background fabric with a very light layer of polyester batting between to make them just the littlest bit puffy (cut the batting with no seam allowance). Some would be tempted to embellish these little flowers with embroidery— French knots or stem stitches—but they would not be suitable for the quilt's intended use. The backing of the quilt is muslin.

The exquisite quilting fills the background of the white squares with tiny stitches forming intricate leaf and wreath patterns. Notice the lovely quilting on the borders—the way the stems of leaves meet in the center, forming a left side and a right side. This takes no more time to stitch; it just takes the pre-planning and execution of an eye tuned to detail!

The lesson here is that even a small project is deserving of attention to detail. This is a quilt that will be handled and loved by many people, so it is only fitting that the work on it should be the very finest.

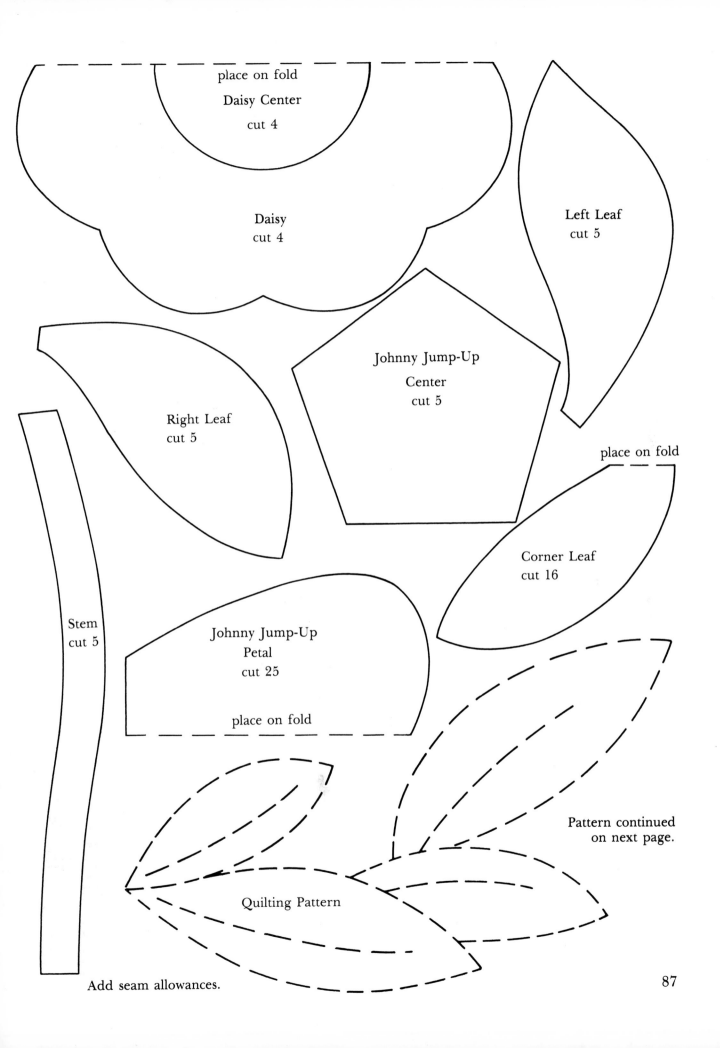

place on fold

Daisy Center
cut 4

Daisy
cut 4

Left Leaf
cut 5

Right Leaf
cut 5

Johnny Jump-Up
Center
cut 5

place on fold

Corner Leaf
cut 16

Stem
cut 5

Johnny Jump-Up
Petal
cut 25

place on fold

Pattern continued
on next page.

Quilting Pattern

Add seam allowances.

87

Continuation of
Johnny Jump-Up.

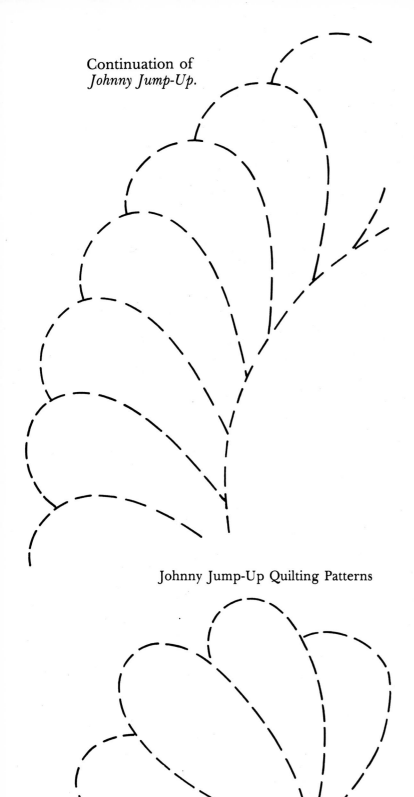

Johnny Jump-Up Quilting Patterns

Peony

(Photograph on page 42.)

From the collection of Dick and Marti Michell; Atlanta, Georgia.

Measure for Measure *(finished sizes)*
Finished quilt: 78″ x 78″
Figured blocks: 7″ x 7″
Plain blocks: 7″ x 7″
Borders: 14″ wide all around
Diamond strips: 4½″ wide
Plain strips: 5″ wide

No book of flower quilts would be worth its salt if it didn't include a pattern for a peony. This fabulous flower with the feathery center has intrigued gardeners and artists for centuries. The tree peony was cultivated in China and Japan from the beginning of civilization but was not introduced into England until 1789, although the bush, or herbaceous, peony was in England as early as 1548.

The peony's colors run the spectrum of purest white to deepest magenta and crimson, and each blossom is framed with a circlet of green sepal leaves. Many people claim the peony to be their favorite flower and look forward to spring and great bouquets of these fragrant, showy blossoms.

The maker of this quilt stayed with a pink and green color scheme, although she has occasionally had to substitute a scrap of blue where green fabric should have been used. The pink fabrics used for the flowers include a tiny abstract print and scraps of pink and white check, as well as one or two other pinkish-red prints. All of these combine to create an effect of feathery pink peonies.

There are many variations of the Peony pattern, and it is often confused with the Carolina Lily (see "Grow Your Own Flower Quilts" for a discussion of the differences). Our example is typical of most Peony designs in that it is pieced very much like a star, but one diamond of the star is omitted and a stem is appliquéd in its place. In some other Peony patterns, the star is complete with all eight points, and the stem is appliquéd at the discretion of the quiltmaker. No matter how you design your peony, the placement of color is of paramount importance, because without

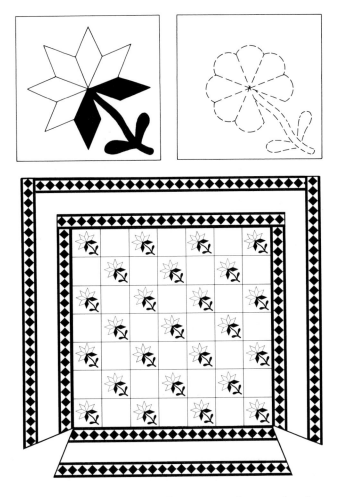

Quality workmanship is exhibited in the quilting of the well chosen designs. A feather cable fills the white section of the border, and a flower with seven rounded petals decorates each white block. These little flowers are stitched freehand just as the peonies are appliquéd freehand; therefore, they don't fit exactly the same way each time.

The bottom corners are cut and bound with a narrow ¼″-wide binding as is the rest of the quilt. Apparently, the corners were done at the same time the quilt was made. No doubt it was planned perfectly to fit a specific bed.

This is surely one of the most charming peony quilts to be found. Check our Recommended Reading and Supplier's Index for others.

the fringe of green leaves underneath the blossom, the flower will look like a star.

In this quilt there is an interesting variety in the shape of the appliquéd leaves. While most are a simple rounded leaf, occasionally one is tri-lobed, or made to look like a bud, or shaped like an oak leaf. Each shape was apparently chosen purely at the whim of the maker.

The borders on this quilt are exceptional. Bands of 1½″ pink diamonds are positioned between 1″ pink bands. These bands flank a solid white 5″ strip to form a complex border which is used on all four sides.

The white backing is pieced in several places to obtain the necessary size. The coarsely woven texture leads one to guess the backing fabric was actually cut from old feed sacks. The filler is cotton and the dark specks which still remain indicate a lower grade of cotton. The impression one gleans from this is that the maker's talent for design and skill with a needle far exceeded her material resources.

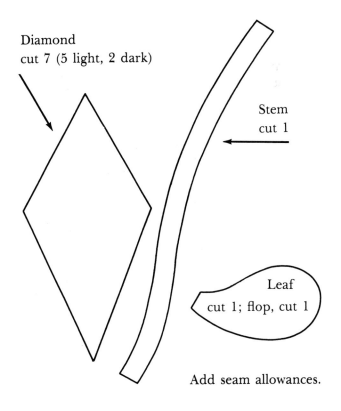

Diamond
cut 7 (5 light, 2 dark)

Stem
cut 1

Leaf
cut 1; flop, cut 1

Add seam allowances.

Grandmother's Flower Garden

(Photograph on page 41.)

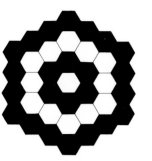

Top two quilts owned by Jeanette Norman Middleton; Greenville, Alabama.

Blue and yellow quilt made by her maternal grandmother, Lucy Catherine Theresa Davis Smith; Fort Deposit, Alabama; 1930-1931.

Green and pink quilt made by her mother, Theodosia Smith Norman and aunt, Lena Belle Gertrude Smith, Fort Deposit, Alabama; 1938-1940.

Quilt in foreground owned and made by Mary Frances Owensby; Linden, Alabama; 1960; with some help from her sister, Sarah Underwood; Unionville, Missouri. Quilted by two anonymous sisters in Arrow Rock, Missouri.

This most popular of patterns comes from "a long way back." Patterns and directions were published as early as 1835, and ever since quiltmakers have accepted its challenge and turned out thousands of these quilts. The basic building blocks for *Grandmother's Flower Garden* are hexagons. Sometimes the sides of the hexagons are as tiny as ⅝" (quilt in the foreground of our photo shows ⅝" hexagons), or as big as 5" across. This pattern is built by adding concentric rings of color to a center, one hexagon at a time. In the past the "English paper liner system" was used since perfectly fitting one hexagon into the angle made by two others is difficult even if the hexagons are large. This involved cutting a paper hexagon for each fabric hexagon. The paper hexagon was cut without seam allowances and was placed in the center of the wrong side of the fabric hexagon. The fabric seam allowances were pressed under to the wrong side and basted to the paper. The edges of the hexagon were then invisibly stitched together.

The Victorians were the last to use the paper liner system—in their wonderful silk and satin "honeycomb" quilts. The flower garden became a favorite pattern for utility quilts, those that were used and washed and used again. When made in a cotton fabric, the flower garden quilts were very durable, primarily because the outline of each hexagon was quilted, thereby holding the batting firmly in place.

We chose as our examples of *Grandmother's Flower Garden* a pair of quilts made by a mother and two daughters, and a vanity piece made of the tiniest hexagons.

First, the pair of quilts. The Black-eyed Susan quilt is the older quilt by some seven to nine years. It is likely the two daughters saw this quilt in progress because their own pink and green quilt is almost identical. In each flower the centers are the same color, surrounded by a row of petals, again the same color in all the flowers, and the third rows in both quilts are various printed fabrics. The pathways are blue on one quilt and green on the other. The color schemes work well because they focus the eye on the flowers.

In both quilts the size of the hexagon building block is 1¼" and there are 1,304 whole hexagons in each quilt.

Measure for Measure (*finished sizes*)

Finished quilt: 70″ x 88″

Blocks: 39 whole blocks

10 filler blocks (3 are cut in half for top and bottom; 7 are cut apart unevenly for sides.)

Hexagons: Colors given for the pink and green quilt. Substitute as required for the Black-eyed Susan.

45 yellow - center

273 pink - first row

588 prints - second row

398 green - pathways

Borders: Use green fabric same as pathways and quilt in a diamond pattern.

Sides: 4″ x 87″ (sew side borders on first; don't miter corners)

Top and bottom: 3¼″ x 61″

Batting: Cotton

Backing: Slightly darker green fabric than the fabric used on front, 71″ x 89″ (allowing ½″ seams)

Binding: ½″ wide, 317″ long. Use the same pink as in the first row of petals.

In the pair of quilts, the individual hexagons are quite respectably small—1¼″ in diameter, and the work is certainly fine. The vanity piece (quilt in foreground of photo), however, shows what can happen when the pattern is refined to a very small unit with sides measuring ⅝″. Although this quilt is only slightly larger than the other two, it contains 6,762 hexagons.

Each flower contains four rows. The centers are solid yellow, surrounded by a ring of six solid-color hexagons. In the third row each hexagon is cut from a flowered print fabric and one of the flowers is centered in each hexagon. Flowers within flowers! Mrs. Owensby undertook the job of piecing this quilt when her sister gave her three completed blocks and a few cut hexagons. She worked on the top for several weeks before "finally" finishing it. After successfully locating more of

the green "silk cotton" for backing, she sent it away to be quilted. The quilt is finished by invisibly hand whipping the backing to the top around all the edges. Notice the absence of borders. The hexagonal shapes make a wonderful pointed finish.

Measure for Measure

Finished quilt: 84″ x 89½″

Blocks: 132 whole blocks, 12 half blocks (used to finish top and bottom)

Hexagons:

Centers - yellow

Row 2 - solid color

Row 3 - print

Row 4 - white

Pathways - green

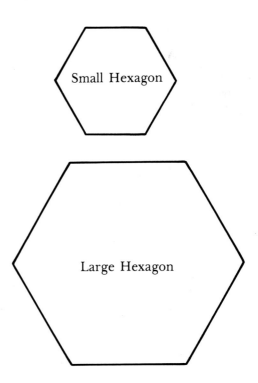

Add seam allowances.

French Nosegay

(Photograph on page 43.)

Owned by Julia Norman; Old Salem, Alabama. Made by her mother, Theodosia Smith Norman and aunt, Lena Belle Gertrude Smith; Fort Deposit, Alabama; 1934.

Measure for Measure *(finished sizes)*

Finished quilt: 75″ x 90″

Whole blocks: 9″ square

Vertical half blocks: 5 for right side; 5 for left side (would equal 5 whole blocks)

Horizontal half blocks: 4 for top; 4 for bottom (would equal 4 whole blocks)

Quarter blocks: 1 each, upper left, upper right, lower left, lower right (would equal 1 whole block)

Border: 3″ wide (green fabric)

Binding: ½″ wide (lavender fabric)

A delightful abstract, this design was inspired by small bouquets of fresh flowers wrapped in green paper. Parisian men traditionally presented these colorful nosegays to the ladies they wished to win. The most colorful and sweetest-smelling flowers such as columbine, phlox, and statice were used in these brightly mixed bouquets. So it is that the "flowers" in this quilted nosegay should be small, bright prints. This quiltmaker chose a color scheme of blues and lavenders, providing a happy harmony to a possible hodge-podge of prints. The prints are from old shirts and dresses of the early 1930s, making the quilt a wonderful repository of old fabrics. Using the same green in the border as the "paper" of the nosegay and using lavender for binding reinforces the color scheme of the nosegay and provides unity of design. The peach background and backing is the best of all possible choices to complete this triadic color scheme of violet, green, and orange.

The piecing of each nosegay is done by hand, as is the diagonal setting together of the blocks. This is very much like piecing the eight-pointed star, and the same problems can develop. To prevent stretching, take care not to handle the bias edges of the pieces any more than absolutely necessary. The English paper-liner system could prove very useful here (see *Grandmother's Flower Garden*, page 90).

Begin setting blocks together by sewing two rows of nine blocks each. One of these rows should have a lower right quarter block at the top and a left half block at the bottom. The other row of nine should have a right half block at the top of the row and an upper left quarter block at the bottom (see diagram). When these two rows of nine are sewed together, you will have your two longest rows completed, and then it will be clear how to sew the remaining blocks together.

Outline quilting is used throughout the quilt. The border is attached by machine and quilted with diagonal lines set 1¼″ apart. The batting of cotton is similar to battings found in many quilts of this period. A ½″ binding, which is machine-sewn to the quilt top, finishes all the edges.

The wonderful old prints, and the patina of time, make this a truly charming piece of history.

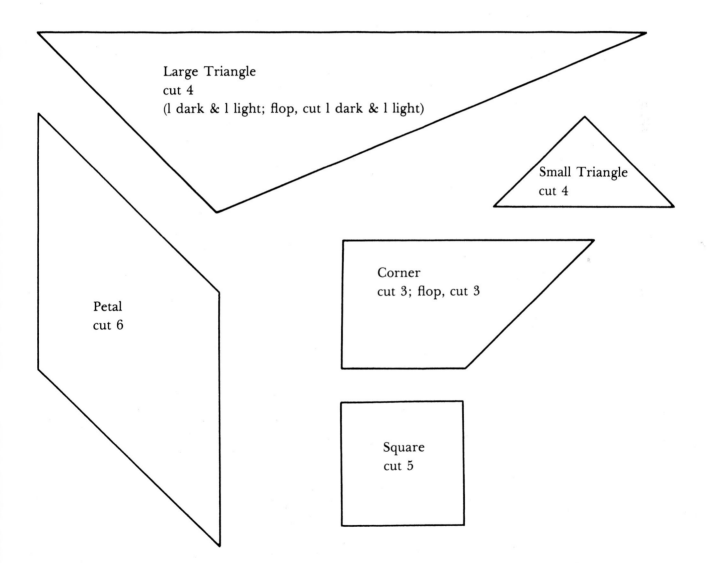

Large Triangle
cut 4
(1 dark & 1 light; flop, cut 1 dark & 1 light)

Small Triangle
cut 4

Petal
cut 6

Corner
cut 3; flop, cut 3

Square
cut 5

Add seam allowances.

Bleeding Heart

(Photograph on page 45.)

Designed, made, and owned by Martha Skelton; Vicksburg, Mississippi; 1980.

Measure for Measure *(finished sizes)*
Finished quilt: 77¼" x 95½"
Blocks: 11½" x 11¼"
Inside white border
   Top and bottom: 4" x 46½"
   Sides: 3" x 75½", quilted with leaves
Pieced border
   4" square
   13 across top and bottom, 20 down
     each side
Green borders
   Top and bottom: 1¼" x 66"
   Sides: 1¼" x 84"
Outside white border
   Top and bottom: 2½" x 70½"
   Sides: 1½" x 86"
Red border
   Top and bottom: 2½" x 77½"
   Sides: 2½" x 95½"
Binding: ½" all around

When Martha Skelton said she was making a bleeding heart quilt, I couldn't imagine what it would be like. She said it was patchwork, but who could have imagined this masterpiece? On close examination, this quilt very definitely represents the flower for which it is named. A real, live bleeding heart explodes at the tip of one blossom into another blossom, and the same feeling is achieved in this quilt in a series of interlocking shapes. The effect is so complex that it takes a few minutes to even discern the basic building block of the pattern.

The mind is teased by the simplicity of the red, green and white color scheme, but simple, it's not. Only one green is used, but there are at least twelve different red prints used! The white fabric is the same throughout. Each block contains a single red print, and some of these prints are repeated again only in the border blocks. The solid red fabric used in the center of each block is not repeated anywhere else in the quilt.

The outline quilting within the body of the piece is ¼" from each seam. The open fan-shaped areas are quilted in concentric rows positioned about 1" apart. These rows of quilting reinforce the circles, which become secondary patterns when the blocks are set together.

A leaf motif is used to quilt the wide white border nearest the inside of the quilt. The leaves point toward the top of the quilt in the side borders and toward the center in the top and bottom borders. The three remaining borders are quilted as one, with diagonal rows placed 2" apart. The five different borders are a beautiful finish to a fabulous quilt.

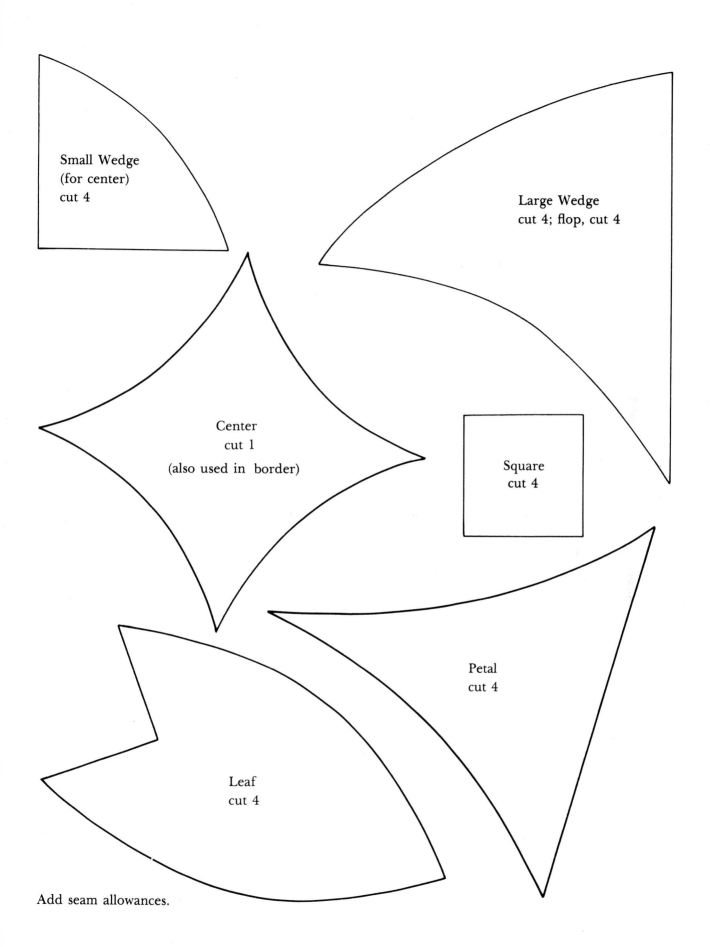

Small Wedge
(for center)
cut 4

Large Wedge
cut 4; flop, cut 4

Center
cut 1
(also used in border)

Square
cut 4

Petal
cut 4

Leaf
cut 4

Add seam allowances.

Bird of Paradise

(Photograph on page 44.)

Owned by Roland and Linda Dickey; Franklin, Alabama.
Made by his mother, Mrs. Clara Dickey; Hueytown, Alabama; 1979.

Measure for Measure *(finished sizes)*
Finished quilt: 95″ x 95″
Blocks: 14½″ x 14½″
Border: 3½″ wide on all sides
Batting: Polyester
Backing: Floral striped cotton/polyester blend
Binding: ½″ all around

We know what you're thinking . . . you've seen this pattern before, but it had a different name. That's certainly possible, because it is also known as *Inverted Tulip, Star and Crescent, Twinkling Star,* and *Dutch Tulip;* then there's *King's Star* and *The King's Crown.* It shows there's not much point in arguing over the name of a quilt, doesn't it? We think it makes a perfect *Bird of Paradise,* sewn in this bright orange mini-dot, especially since the burst of diamond shapes in the center so closely represents the topknot of the "bird."

The impact of the orange and white color scheme works well here to achieve a crisp, clean effect, especially appealing on a summer bed. While we had the quilt out on display, it attracted more attention than some of the other more complicated quilts.

The piecing of each block is done by hand, practically a necessity when this many curves and points must match. You would think that after piecing 36 of these blocks, Mrs. Dickey would have been ready to set them together by machine, but she wasn't. Not only did she set all the blocks together by hand, she sewed the beautifully mitered borders and binding completely by hand too.

Her quilting follows the outline of each shape in the block, and it is placed ¼″ from the seam lines. The addition of a teardrop shape in each corner of the block forms a secondary floral pattern when the blocks are joined together. The borders are quilted with parallel rows of stitching set 1″ apart.

A pretty floral stripe was used for the quilt backing, and a dust ruffle was made out of this fabric, as were some pillows. The quilt block was used on the face of some of the pillows, providing the final detail to a striking overall decorating scheme.

Add seam allowances.

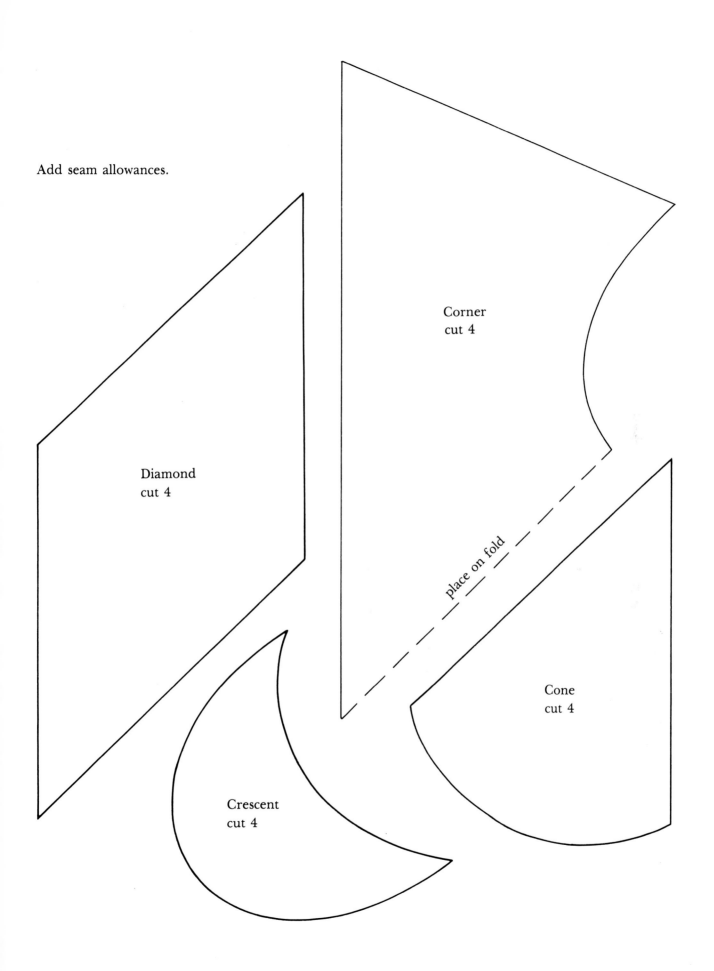

Corner
cut 4

Diamond
cut 4

place on fold

Cone
cut 4

Crescent
cut 4

Dahlia and Basket

(Photograph on page 45.)

From the collection of Robert and Helen Cargo; Tuscaloosa, Alabama.
Provenance of quilt: Wisconsin; c. 1910.

Measure for Measure *(finished sizes)*
Finished quilt: 77" x 77"
Blocks: 13½" x 13½"
Half blocks: 13½" x 13½" x 19" triangle
Quarter blocks: 13½" x 10" x 10" triangle

Who could possibly resist this sweet little Victorian basket with its perfectly delightful dahlia? Although it's firmly rooted in the ground, the dahlia seems in danger of toppling over from the weight of the big bud it carries on its stem. This is a "summer quilt"; that is, a lightweight top that has been hemmed on the edges to provide a clean finish. Many summer quilts are lined and lightly quilted. Some even have a very lightweight batting such as a sheet or cotton blanket. These were easier to quilt than those with no batting at all. A summer quilt was used to make up the bed during summer days and to provide a touch of cover on warm nights. We think it's a great way to "make up" a summer picnic table!

This quilt top is sturdily constructed. The piecing of the baskets is done by hand with very close stitches. Tiny hidden stitches are used to appliqué all the flowers and basket handles.

The flower and leaf are very interesting. At first glance it seems the flower must be completely lined and turned with seam allowances to the inside in order to achieve such perfect curves in the eight lobes or scallops, but that's not the case. It's simply a matter of using the smallest imaginable seam allowance and the tiniest possible stitches. The urge to embellish the center of the flower with embroidery has been resisted. The leaves and ¼" stems are cut in one piece in the original quilt, again requiring supreme skill at appliqué. We have given them as separate pattern pieces here in the hope of making the project easier for you. The stem and the calyx of the bud, fortunately, are not cut in one piece.

The ½"-wide basket handle is cut on the bias, and sewn to the upper triangle of the basket block before the two triangles are attached. The quiltmaker drew a pencil line on the wrong side of the fabric as a placement guide for the top edge of the handle's curve. There are 36 triangles and one square in the body of each basket. After machine stitching all the blocks together the edges are hemmed by machine.

The strength of the piece permits washing and indeed it appears to have been washed more than once. This is a wonderful design, and of course, if you wanted to, you could fill the baskets with more delightful dahlias!

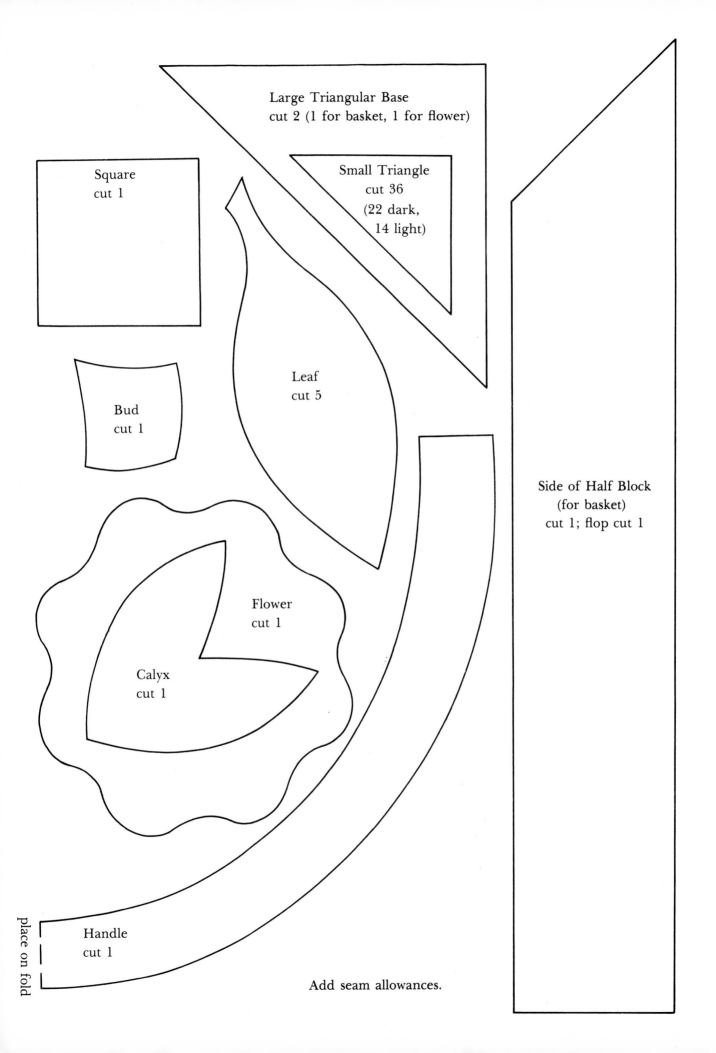

Large Triangular Base
cut 2 (1 for basket, 1 for flower)

Square
cut 1

Small Triangle
cut 36
(22 dark,
14 light)

Leaf
cut 5

Bud
cut 1

Side of Half Block
(for basket)
cut 1; flop cut 1

Flower
cut 1

Calyx
cut 1

place on fold

Handle
cut 1

Add seam allowances.

Centennial Lily

(Photograph on page 44.)

Designed, quilted, and owned by Martha Skelton; Vicksburg, Mississippi: 1980.

Measure for Measure *(finished sizes)*
Finished quilt: 79″ x 97″
Lily blocks: 17½″ square
Filler triangles: 24½″ x 17¼″ x 12¼″
Corner triangles: 17¼″ x 12¼″ x 12¼″
Side borders: 18″ wide, 97″ long
Top border: 7¾″ x 50″
Bottom border: 18″ wide, 78″ across

The skillful touch of a master quilter has never been more evident than in this quilt. Mrs. Skelton's unerring sense of color has brought together two fabrics that would have been turned down by a less experienced and less confident quiltmaker. She has chosen a very strong peach and combined it with a red and yellow calico to make the petals. A dark olive green (with a lot of yellow in it) forms the stems, leaves, and calyx of each flower. The flowers are appliquéd onto muslin, and the edge of the quilt is finished with bias binding. The batting is polyester and the back of the quilt is muslin.

The master's touch is also at work in the borders of *Centennial Lily.* Mrs. Skelton has appliquéd a wonderful twining vine of lilies—was she thinking of the climbing gloriosa when she designed the border? She has reversed the color of the petals in every other flower on the vine. The stem of this vine is cut on the bias. Mrs. Skelton suggests, when working with bias, baste the ¼″ fold on each side of fabric; roll the bias onto a card until you're ready to use it. When you appliqué the vine or stems in place, sew the inside curve first; if you make it lie flat, the outside curve will automatically flatten itself, making it much easier to stitch.

The top and bottom borders vary from the sides. The top border shows a lily bud not quite open. At the center of the bottom border, a single green calyx marks the meeting place of the left and right borders.

After piecing the flowers by hand, Mrs. Skelton used tiny precision stitches to appliqué the flowers and stems onto the muslin background.

The only machine stitches on the quilt are those that join the blocks and triangles together and join the border to the body of the quilt. The bias binding is machine stitched to the top of the quilt, then hand stitched to the backing of the quilt.

The evenness and precision of the quilting, which is almost unbelievable, and the sophistication of the leaf and stem designs combine to make a truly gorgeous quilt.

100

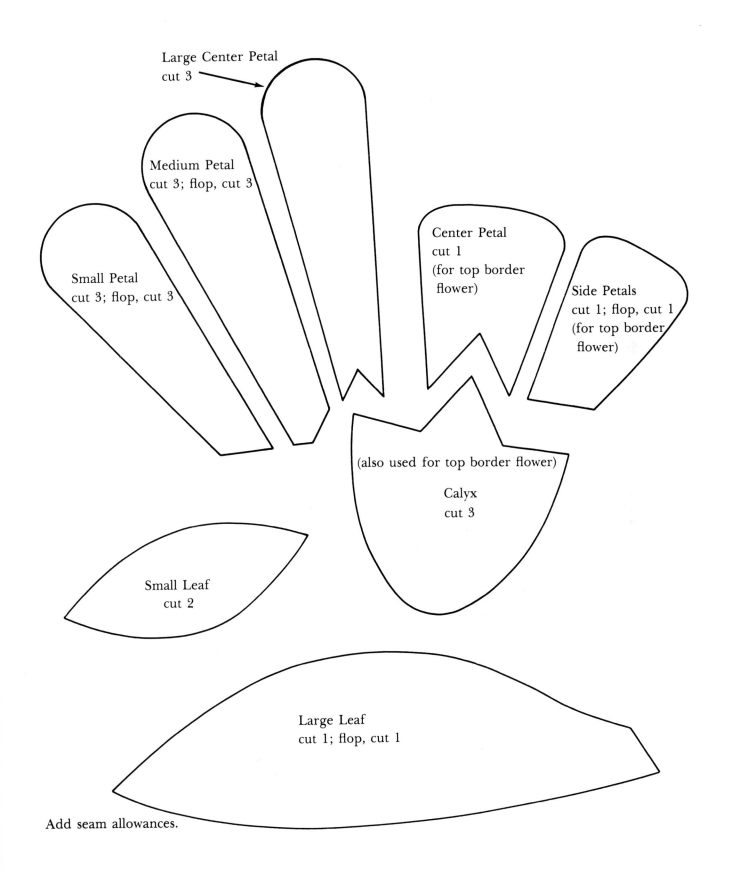

Large Center Petal
cut 3

Medium Petal
cut 3; flop, cut 3

Small Petal
cut 3; flop, cut 3

Center Petal
cut 1
(for top border
flower)

Side Petals
cut 1; flop, cut 1
(for top border
flower)

(also used for top border flower)

Calyx
cut 3

Small Leaf
cut 2

Large Leaf
cut 1; flop, cut 1

Add seam allowances.

Ohio Rose

(Photograph on page 50.)

Owned by Susanne Johnson; Frisco City, Alabama. Made by Nancy Sirmon and her daughter-in-law, Inez Sirmon; Franklin, Alabama; pink quilt, 1949; red quilt, 1959.

Measure for Measure *(finished sizes)*
Finished red quilt: 66" x 83"
Blocks: 17" x 17"
Borders: 7" wide at rosebud, 6½" wide between buds
Binding: ½" wide, green

Finished pink quilt: 67" x 83"
Blocks: 16" x 16"
Borders: 9" wide
Binding: ½" wide

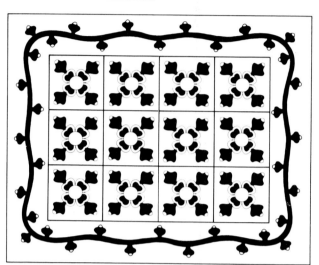

As the pioneers moved westward, the *Tudor Rose* or *Whig Rose* of the New World became the *Ohio Rose* commemorating that migration. As settlers moved even farther west, the name changed to *Prairie Rose*. Since quilters always call a pattern by the name it had when they met it, there still remains an *Ohio Rose*; however, as these two examples prove, it has many variations.

At first glance, these quilts seem very much alike. Rows of roses with bold faces made of layered, lobed petals march across the quilts. Each rose shows four buds, and these same buds are repeated in the border.

The color scheme, of course, is one of the most obvious differences, but there are others. The red rose has two separate green leaves behind its bud; the pink one has the leaves cut as one with the bud. The border treatment is also different. But perhaps the most significant difference in the two is in the central, main blossom. Both blossoms are made up of three layers: two separate layers of petals and a center circle. The four separate red petals and center of the red rose are placed on a solid piece of pale pink fabric which represents the outer layer of petals. In the pink rose pattern, the two layers of petals are shaped exactly the same, with a distinctive heart shape. Each of the petals is cut and appliquéd separately. The center circle is appliquéd to cover the juncture of the petals.

Both roses are outline quilted, and in the red rose the open areas are filled with diamonds similar to the shape of the bud. The spaces between the buds on the border are filled with lily-like shapes. The backing of this quilt is pale pink; batting is cotton. In the pink quilt, the seams where the blocks are joined are stitched with double circles and tiny ovals. It's a good guess that some household object, such as a jar, bottle, or dish, was traced for these rather curious designs. The border is quilted in rows, spaced ½" apart, which follow the curving of the vine. The backing of this quilt is the same green as the buds and the binding.

Even though these two *Ohio Roses* are made by the same two women, there are a lot of differences. In fact, you need two different sets of patterns!

Add seam allowances.

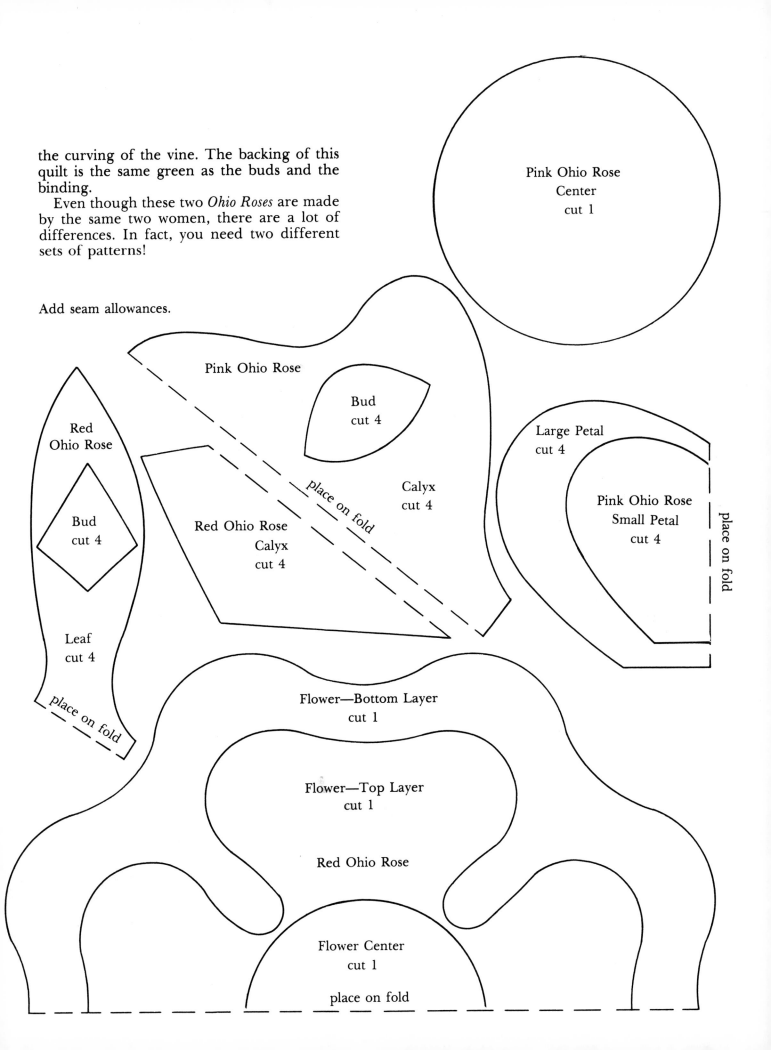

Pink Ohio Rose
Center
cut 1

Pink Ohio Rose

Bud
cut 4

Calyx
cut 4

Large Petal
cut 4

Pink Ohio Rose
Small Petal
cut 4

place on fold

Red
Ohio Rose

Bud
cut 4

Red Ohio Rose
Calyx
cut 4

place on fold

Leaf
cut 4

place on fold

Flower—Bottom Layer
cut 1

Flower—Top Layer
cut 1

Red Ohio Rose

Flower Center
cut 1

place on fold

Rose and Bird

(Photograph on page 51.)

From the collection of Dick and Marti Michell; Atlanta, Georgia.

Measure for Measure *(finished sizes)*
Finished quilt: 66½″ x 87½″
Motifs: 20½″ x 20½″
Border: 7″ wide
Sashing: 5½″ wide
Binding: ¼″

This wonderful design appears to be the result of the quiltmaker taking her favorite part from a number of quilt patterns and combining them all into one happy whole. There's a touch of *Rose of Sharon,* a bit of *Whig Rose,* a hint of *Triple Rose,* a bud that could be drawn from *Ohio Rose,* and then, finally a pair of birds for good measure!

She's also combined techniques, using appliqué, patchwork, and, of course, superior quilting. Clearly, a very experienced needlewoman was at work on this piece!

The central flower is a combination of patchwork and appliqué. An elongated diamond or four-pointed star at the very center of the block is set with an appliquéd circle. The same fabric of the circle is used to fill in the edges of the star shape to form a larger circle. The outer two rows are pieced from thumb-nail petal shapes. The inside petals, cut from a tiny pink and white check, alternate with red clamshells.

At four points equally positioned around the clamshell petals, a Whig Rose leaf shape of a tiny green calico is attached. This leaf shape has been embellished with an appliquéd circle, just like the center circle.

The remaining four clamshell petals have sprouted wonderful branches, each bearing two flowers and four leaves. The scalloped edges of these solid red flowers with their appliquéd centers give the suggestion that they are emerging into full-blown blossoms.

Six of these large motifs have been meticulously appliquéd onto background blocks, then set together with a 5½″ wide sashing. There is a row of sashing down the center and down one side of the quilt, but it is missing at each end and the other side. If we accept that the quilt could be wider than it is long, the

sashing makes more sense. It shows that the quilt was made for a short, wide bed. The white sashing at the top of the quilt allows a tuck-under for pillows.

The delightful border is made up of a twining vine on which birds are perching and buds are beginning to burst into bloom. The birds are positioned on top of the vine, and the buds sprout from beneath the vine. A few leaves, different from those with the flowers, grow here and there. The basic unit of the border consists of a pair of birds facing one another, four leaves and two buds. Notice the birds are not only different colors; they may even be different species! The entire head of one is red, while another has a red dot on top of his head.

The basic unit is repeated around the quilt until reaching the corners. Apparently, the quiltmaker decided to work in a little variety here, because no two corners are the same! Each of her four solutions, however, seems effective, and she could have used any one of them for all the corners.

The backing is the same white as the background fabric, and the cotton batting is quite thin, probably from its many washings.

Surprisingly, the quilt does not display a myriad of quilting designs. As inventive as the

104

maker was with pattern, it seems that she must have used some self-control in limiting the background to ½″ squares. Each appliquéd shape is closely and beautifully outline quilted inside and outside, so the back side of the quilt looks like it's been made of trapunto. It's fabulous! Each vine, although only a scant ½″ wide, has been stitched with four rows of quilting. Even the little birds appear in complete detail! There is no area larger than ½″ square that is not quilted.

Add seam allowances.

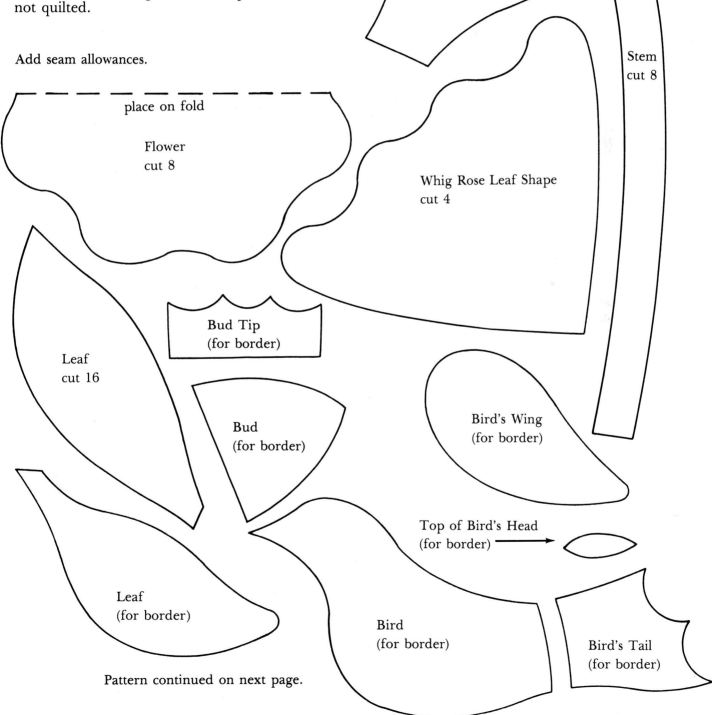

place on fold

Calyx
(for border)

Stem
cut 8

Flower
cut 8

Whig Rose Leaf Shape
cut 4

Leaf
cut 16

Bud Tip
(for border)

Bud
(for border)

Bird's Wing
(for border)

Top of Bird's Head
(for border)

Leaf
(for border)

Bird
(for border)

Bird's Tail
(for border)

Pattern continued on next page.

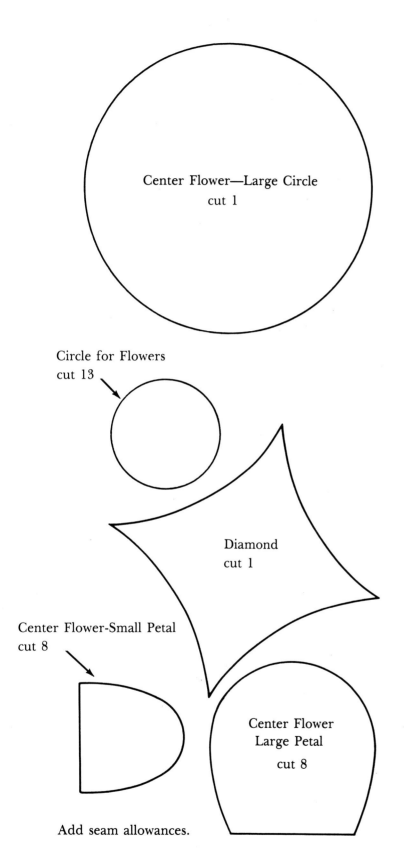

Center Flower—Large Circle
cut 1

Circle for Flowers
cut 13

Diamond
cut 1

Center Flower-Small Petal
cut 8

Center Flower
Large Petal
cut 8

Add seam allowances.

Rose Wreath

(Photograph on page 46.)
Owned by Sally Beatrice Barber;
Montgomery, Alabama.
Made by her sister-in-law's mother, Mrs. Sallie
Knight; Clio, Alabama; 1930.

Measure for Measure *(finished sizes)*
Finished quilt: 76″ x 91″
Blocks: 15″ x 15″
Border: 7½″ wide
Binding: ½″ wide

The roses of this pattern, shaped as they are into a circle with pink-tipped buds sprouting among the leaves, seem to be the visualization of that famous phrase, "Rose is a rose is a rose is a rose." The implicit meaning of the wreath shape — just as it has no beginning, it has no end—might also apply to the unending beauty of roses. You will surely believe this when you see the 80 flowers that make up the 20 wreaths on this quilt!

Even though this quilt was made over a half-century ago, the colors are not faded, but are as bright and cheerful as the day they were cut and stitched. The three shades of rose used have such subtle differences in color that they almost escape the eye. The darker shade rings the yellow center, followed by the medium shade, and finally the lighter shade. The medium shade is so nearly the darker shade, yet so nearly the lighter shade, that it seems to blend with both, and all three contrast nicely with the creamy white background. The effect is very much like an actual rose on the vine — the outer petals in many varieties lighten with age.

This is another of the "layered roses," made of shaped pieces stacked on top of one another. There is no additional batting used between the layers of petals, but a dimensional effect is still obtained.

The best way to begin work for this project is to draw the 10″ circle lightly onto the background fabric, then trace the leaves and outer row of petals onto the circle. The leaves and buds are stitched down first, then the ⅜″-wide bias for the stem, and finally the flowers. Mrs. Knight's appliqué stitches are almost invisible in attaching all of these pieces. Each block has sixteen leaves, four buds, and four flowers.

The flower shape with all the layers of petals is repeated in the quilting at the center of each block and at the corners where the blocks are joined. Additionally, each layer of the appliquéd flowers is quilted. The stem and leaf shapes are outlined, and the joining seams of the blocks are quilted ¼″ to either side. The border is quilted in groups of three rows of straight stitches set ¾″ apart, and spaced 1¼″ from the next group.

The backing, borders, and binding are medium pink. The edges are shaped with shallow, 1¾″-deep scallops that measure 6½″ from notch to notch.

Viewed from the backing side, this *Rose Wreath* quilt looks almost like a whole cloth quilt done in bright pink with white stitching.

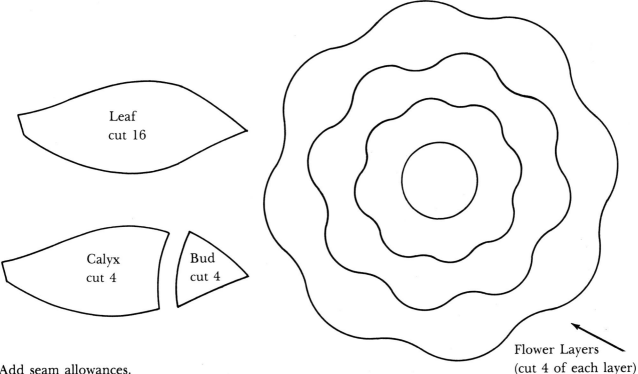

Leaf
cut 16

Calyx
cut 4

Bud
cut 4

Flower Layers
(cut 4 of each layer)

Add seam allowances.

Victorian Rose

(Photograph on page 49.)

Designed, made and owned by Mary Frances Owensby; Linden, Alabama; 1962. Quilted by an anonymous woman in Missouri, who was 82 years old when she worked this piece.

Measure for Measure *(finished sizes)*
Finished quilt: 92½" x 99"
Center square: 23¼" x 23¼"

The longer you look at this quilt, the more you love it! The vanilla and strawberry ice cream colors are restful and soothing, and the more you look at the two colors together, the better match they seem to be! The single rose in the center of the quilt seems the perfect choice for the only touch of color. This restraint of color and pattern is played against what seems to have been joyful abandon in the use of elaborate borders and quilting patterns! There are eight different borders and innumerable quilting designs, making this quilt a veritable encyclopedia of quilting patterns. If you're one of those people who loves to quilt more than you like to piece or appliqué, this is definitely your cup of tea!

The central motif is a simple rose composed of four layers of scallop-edged petals, with the darker color in the center graduating to the lighter color on the outside. The center is embellished with a random scattering of golden French knots. Four branches, each bearing five leaves, are a soft green color with a slight blue cast.

The patchwork Sawtooth pattern is sewn in three different places in the interior borders. The half vanilla, half strawberry building block of the Sawtooth border is 2½" wide, and some 475 inches are needed to make all three of the interior borders in the quilt. It would certainly be a good idea to make all the Sawtooth at once, so that you can have it ready to stitch into the quilt when you begin assembly.

The diamond point finish of the edges alternates a vanilla triangle with a strawberry triangle. These points are made from 2½" squares of fabric folded in half on the diagonal, then in half again, so that a 1½" x 1½" x 3" triangle is formed. The 3" edge is laid on the seam line between the quilted top and the backing before the backing is permanently stitched in place (see "Grow Your Own Flower Quilts"). There are 105 diamond points used to finish three edges of this quilt—the top edge is left plain. A vanilla-colored cotton backing is used, which Mrs. Owensby whipped to the quilt front after turning under a ¼" edge.

The eight borders showcase a wide variety of quilting designs—cables, diamonds, intertwined circles. Decide on the number and width of borders you will need and use these same quilting patterns or substitute your favorites to make your own sampler different from Mrs. Owensby's!

See *Ohio Rose* for a description of the quilt at the foot of the bed.

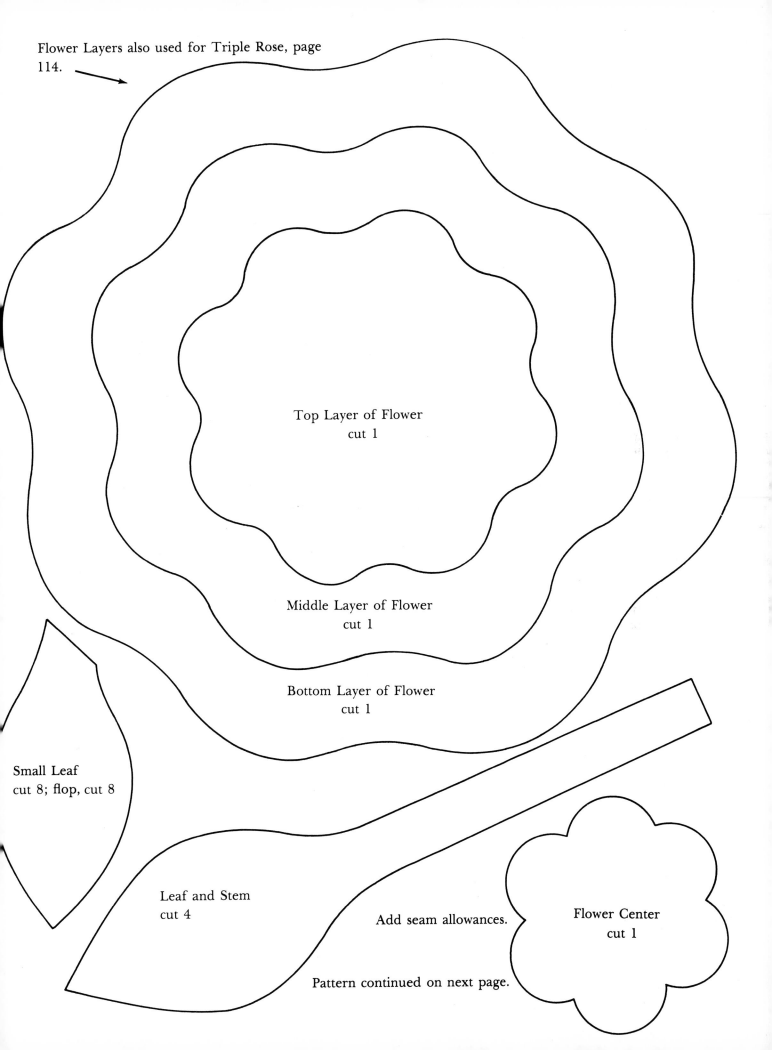

Flower Layers also used for Triple Rose, page 114.

Top Layer of Flower
cut 1

Middle Layer of Flower
cut 1

Bottom Layer of Flower
cut 1

Small Leaf
cut 8; flop, cut 8

Leaf and Stem
cut 4

Add seam allowances.

Flower Center
cut 1

Pattern continued on next page.

Whig Rose

(Photograph on page 48.)

From the collection of Dick and Marti Michell; Atlanta, Georgia.

Measure for Measure *(finished sizes)*
Finished quilt: Approximately 82″ x 82″
Motifs: Approximately 27″ square
Borders: Green 1″ wide, blue with appliqué
    swags 12½″ wide

Of all the quilt patterns named for roses, the *Whig Rose* is one of the most elusive to pin down. An explanation, according to Orlofsky in *Quilts In America,* is that in the 1840s, the Whigs and the Democrats each claimed the pattern as their own; therefore, a *Whig Rose* and a *Democrat Rose* had different names but the same pattern. The dispute was never settled, but as Orlofsky points out, in 1844 when the Whig candidate, Henry Clay, was beaten by the Democrat, James K. Polk, the pattern named *Whig's Defeat* left no room for question!

Most patterns identified as *Whig Rose* have four leaf-like shapes behind the central flower. These shapes could possibly represent a palm leaf, a bristle, or scraps of ribbon—perhaps a symbol of the pattern's political origin. This integral shape also resembles a Maltese cross. Often, a branch sprouts from between the leaf-like shapes, bearing all sorts of leaves and buds and secondary flowers.

This *Whig Rose* is an outstanding example with its four large motifs. The center of the quilt is set with the same yellow and pink "rose" found in the center of each motif. This central flower is one of the "layered" rose designs, and it works well with the daisy-like flower on the branches. Remarkably, the branches bear both pink and yellow buds!

The fabric choices are interesting. Each color is actually a tiny print. The blue and white print is an unusual choice for a background, and it makes a distinctive quilt. The backing of the quilt is a cheerful red and white striped fabric, with stripes about ⅛″ wide. Binding is a red knit, ¼″ wide, the type manufactured in the early 1960s.

The center square measures approximately 56″. The background fabric is not pieced, making one think perhaps it was a sheet. To position the motifs, divide the square into fourths by basting or lightly pressing a guide. Draw the shapes of the appliqué onto the background fabric to facilitate perfect placement of design.

It is worth noting how essential the 1″ border of green is to the design. It provides the only linear element. It's the framework which stabilizes the design because every other line in the quilt is curved.

The swags and tassels of the border remind one of the bunting used to dress a campaign stage—a humorous nod to the quilt's political beginnings. The swags are not big, 6″ across and 3″ deep. The tassels are cut from a single piece of fabric and are only 3″ long, the smallest pieces in the quilt. There are more tassels than any other piece; in fact, there are 44 of them on the border. Nothing fazes a determined quiltmaker!

Quilting follows the shape of each piece. Indeed, it is difficult to see the quilting from the top of the quilt, because it is placed so close to the edge of the appliqué it is almost hidden. The green border is quilted with a single cable

Pattern continued on next page.

111

pattern and the swags are filled with rows quilted approximately ¾″ apart. The background of the whole quilt is stitched with pairs of diagonal lines set ¼″ apart and 1″ from the next pair. The leaf-like shapes are quilted from the deep "v" of the outer edge to the base.

This pattern is not terribly difficult. Although there are lots of curves, the pieces are big, and the curves and points are more easily appliquéd here than on smaller pieces. The most difficult part will be piecing the two outer rows of petals on the rose before appliquéing them in place. There are 13 petals on each row, with one row of petals larger than the other. Of course, the tassels will take time, but if a pressing guide is made before appliqué is begun, the process will be speeded up.

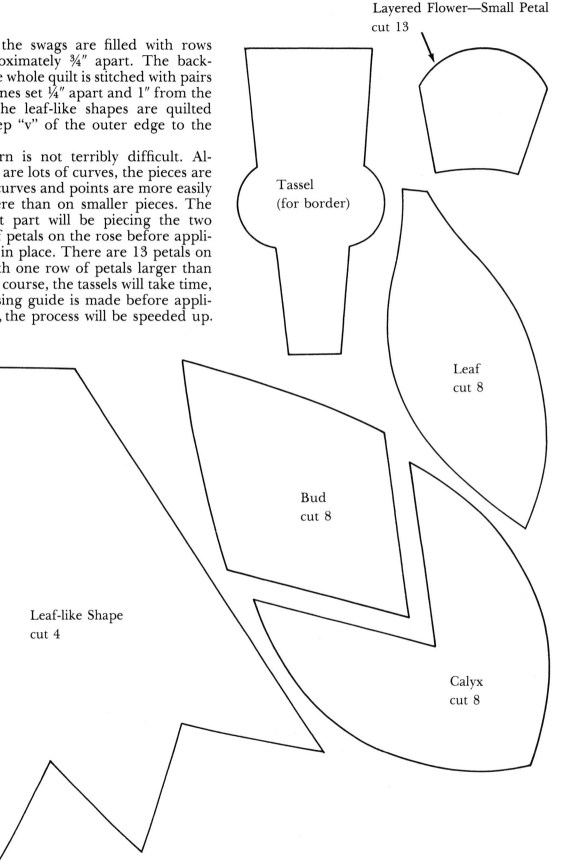

Layered Flower—Small Petal
cut 13

Tassel
(for border)

Leaf
cut 8

Bud
cut 8

place on fold

Leaf-like Shape
cut 4

Calyx
cut 8

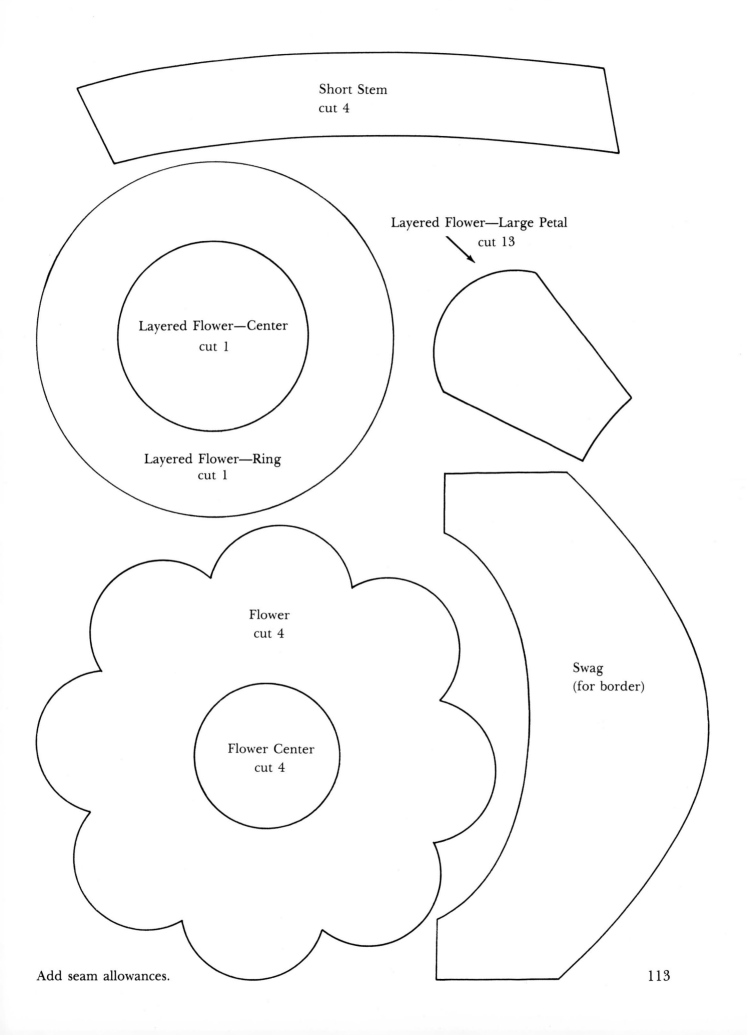

Short Stem
cut 4

Layered Flower—Large Petal
cut 13

Layered Flower—Center
cut 1

Layered Flower—Ring
cut 1

Flower
cut 4

Flower Center
cut 4

Swag
(for border)

Add seam allowances.

113

Triple Rose

(Photograph on page 51.)

Owned by Mrs. Mary Frances Owensby; Linden, Alabama.
Made by her sister, Mrs. Julia Putnam; Marshall, Missouri; 1917.
Quilted by two anonymous sisters in Iowa.

Measure for Measure *(finished sizes)*
Finished quilt: 89½" x 89½"
Blocks: 20" x 20"
Border: 14½" wide
Binding: ¼" wide

This wedding quilt was made in 1917 for Mrs. Owensby by her sister. With blushing pinks set against a pristine white, it reminds us of a bride, and the swags of the border suggest the train of the bride's wedding dress. Even the greenery, with its distinctively notched edges, looks like the ferns and palms so often chosen for wedding decorations.

The fabrics used are polished cotton sateen, which means that the quilt has a very pretty overall sheen. Three shades of pink are used for each blossom, with the lighter pink forming the outer row of petals. A very unusual gray-green makes up the leaf and bud shapes. Mrs. Owensby says the green fabric has not changed color over the years—this was the original color. There are two white fabrics used for background fabric; one is a creamy white and the other a blue-white.

Feathered plumes are quilted around each rose bud, forming a partial oval. A quilted feathered wreath, filled with ½" squares, was chosen to fill the open areas where the blocks are joined. At even intervals along the seams joining the squares, three diamonds are quilted giving us the impression of a leaf. The wide borders, decorated with graceful swags draping from the rosebuds, are quilted with 1" diamonds.

The backing is also white cotton. The binding is green, and the batting is cotton.

What a thoughtful gift—a quilt designed by one sister for another!

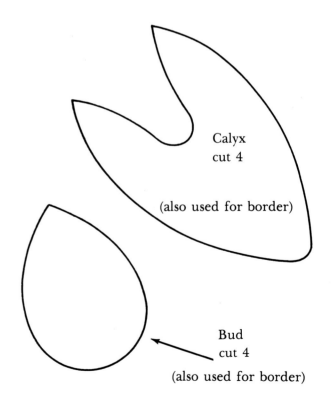

Calyx
cut 4

(also used for border)

Bud
cut 4

(also used for border)

114

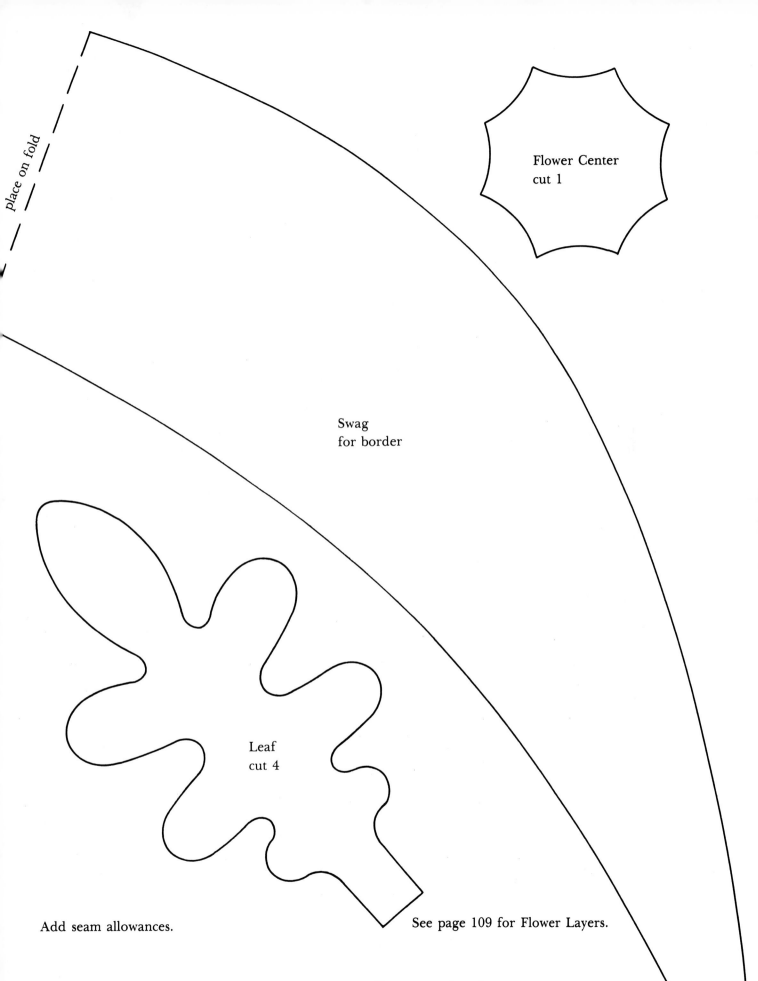

place on fold

Flower Center
cut 1

Swag
for border

Leaf
cut 4

Add seam allowances.

See page 109 for Flower Layers.

Pattern continued on next page.

Continuation of *Triple Rose.*

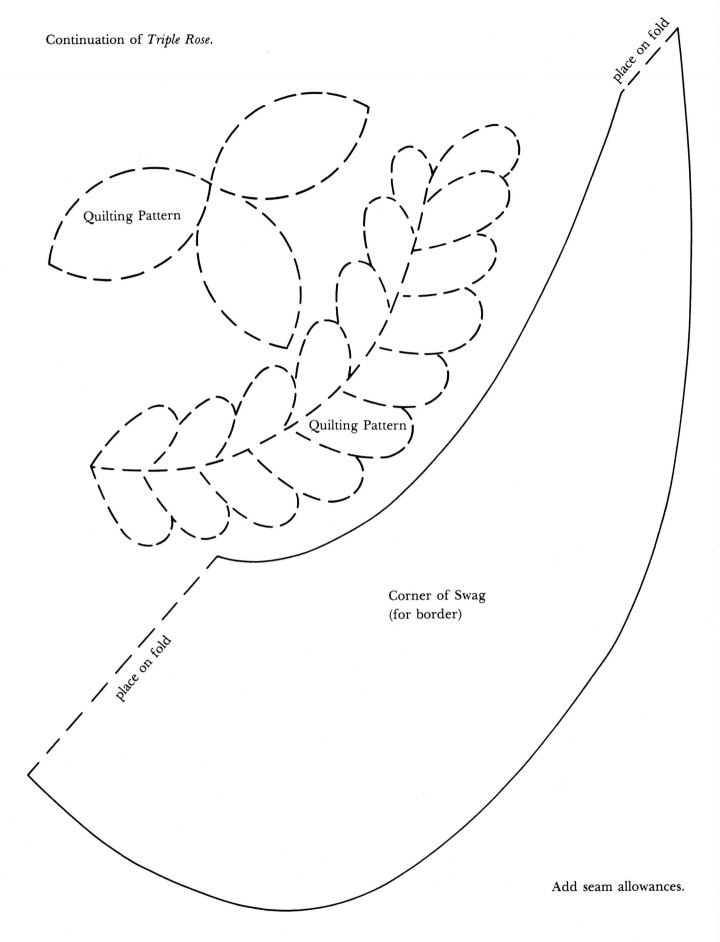

place on fold

Quilting Pattern

Quilting Pattern

place on fold

Corner of Swag
(for border)

Add seam allowances.

116

Tropicana Medallion

(Photograph on page 47.)

Designed and made by Sandra Sandberg for the Fairfield Processing Corporation Contest; Danbury, Connecticut, 1980.

Measure for Measure *(finished sizes)*

Finished quilt: 84″ x 84″

Center square: 39½″ x 39½″

Fabric requirements for 45″ wide cotton/polyester blend:

    Off-white solid; 1¼ yards

    Dark orange print; 2 yards

    Medium orange print; 1¾ yards

    Light orange solid; ¾ yard

    Blue-green print; 2¼ yards

    Beige print; 2 yards

    Backing fabric of your choice; 5 yards

    Binding: 10 yards, 2″-wide bias tape or strips

Here's a terrific quilt that packs a lot of punch and is fun to make. The idea of making one big, knock-your-eyes-out block and surrounding it with six borders of varying widths means that you won't become bored because of repetition. The quilt will be finished before you have done anything twice! The first two borders near the center of the quilt are the same on all four sides, but after that, the borders switch colors as they go around the center.

The color scheme is a little unusual in that a blue-green print fabric was used in the places you would expect a true green. As you can see in the color photograph, the leaves of the live rose definitely have a blue cast. So the color is not as far from nature as we might think. The peachy-orange of the other prints reminds us of the beloved Tropicana Rose.

Because of the size of this motif, it is impossible to give you a full-size pattern. The flower is drawn on a grid with instructions for enlarging. If you've never enlarged a pattern from a grid before, this is a good pattern to get you started. Don't overlook the potential of this design for stenciling and smaller appliqué projects. It's a great design to use to decorate an entire room!

After you've enlarged the pattern, you need to make full-size paper patterns for each shape. Then cut the following pieces for the blossom:

One 40″ square from off-white fabric

Two leaves and one stem from blue-green print

Eight pieces from solid light orange fabric (labeled L1 to L8 on pattern)

Nine pieces from dark orange print (labeled 1-9)

One piece from medium orange print the shape of the entire rose (excluding leaves)

The border strips are cut as follows:

Beige print fabric

    Four 40½″ x 1½″ strips (B1)

    Two 63″ x 3″ strips (B2)

    Two 69″ x 3″ strips (B3)

Dark orange print

    Two 54″ x 6″ strips (D1)

    Two 63″ x 3″ strips (D2)

Medium orange print

    Two 54″ x 6″ strips (M1)

    Two 69″ x 3″ strips (M2)

Blue-green print

    Four 45″ x 3″ strips (G1)

    Four 78″ x 6″ strips (G2)

Pattern continued on next page.

To appliqué the rose, turn under all edges of all pieces and baste in place. Center the big medium orange print piece, the leaves and the stem on the background square. Pin down, baste, and appliqué. Remove basting. Then place the dark orange print pieces and the light orange pieces in place according to the drawing. Pin down, baste in place, and appliqué. Remove all basting when finished.

To make the borders, join strips around center appliquéd square with ¼″ seams. Begin with B1 strips. Stitch a B1 strip to the top edge of the center square, so that ½″ of the strip extends to the right of the square. Seam another B1 strip along the right edge of the square, joining this second strip to the extension of the first. In similar fashion, add B1 strips to the bottom and left edges of the square, so that the spiraling strips form a border around the center square. Next add a similar spiraling border of four G1 strips. Continue increasing the border, and following the photograph for color placement. The final border is formed by four G2 strips. This completes the assembly of the quilt top, and now it's ready to be pressed from the wrong side.

The rose is outline quilted around each shape, and a "vein" is stitched down the center of each leaf. The borders are quilted in straight lines, beginning ¾″ from the innermost seam and continuing every 1½″ thereafter, always following the direction of the border.

How to Work with a Pattern
To Enlarge:
● Prepare a grid to the scale of the pattern. For example, if each square equals 3″, prepare a grid of 3″ squares.

● Number squares vertically and horizontally on both the pattern and your grid. Use the numbers as a guide to copy the pattern outline from the original, square by square.

To Transfer:
● Use dressmaker's carbon for all types of fabric. Use carbon or graphite paper for other materials.

● When transferring the design, keep the article flat and smooth. Place transfer medium on the article, position the pattern on transfer medium, and secure it with pins, tape, or other suitable means. Trace with pencil, pen, or tracing wheel.

● If the article is transparent, simply lay it over the pattern, secure, and trace. If the article is translucent, tape the article over the pattern on a window or light box and trace.

Note: Pencils and pens which iron on or transfer by rubbing are available through fabric, needlework, or craft shops.

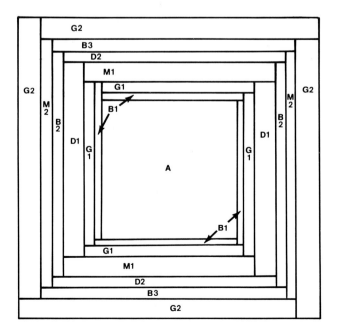

Each square equals 3″.

Rose of Sharon

(Photograph on page 48.)

From the collection of Robert and Helen Cargo; Tuscaloosa, Alabama.
Provenance of quilt: Kentucky; 1900-1910.

Measure for Measure *(finished sizes)*
Finished quilt: 84″ x 95″
Blocks: 21″ x 21″
Top and bottom borders: 15″ x 63″
Side borders: 10″ x 93″
Batting: Cotton
Backing: White cotton
Binding: ¼″

This quiltmaker must have agreed with the poetry of John Lyly, " A rose is sweeter in the budde than full blowne," because, including the great big ones at the end of the branches, she has 16 "buddes" in her main block. In fact, the center flower seems relatively insignificant compared to the profusion of buds, which she used not only in the main body of the quilt— but in the borders too!

We know something about this woman besides the fact that she loved rosebuds—she also had amazing patience! She had to cut yards and yards and yards of bias to make the stems and vines for the border. With the addition of the beautifully planned borders and their different buds and tiny blossoms, the quilt shows a profusion of wonderful floral shapes.

There are nine blocks in this finished quilt. The borders at the top and bottom are set in between the side borders; because they are different widths, mitering would have been difficult. The twining vines of the side borders create ovals which are 6″ wide and 9″ long. The ovals on the top and bottom borders are 12″ wide and 15″ long. The quilt design is not limited to one direction. The roses go up one side and down the other, and the design forms a mirror image at the center of the top and bottom borders.

A combination of patchwork and appliqué was used in constructing the quilt. The center flowers, which contain 24 pieces, are patched together before being applied, and the large corner buds are worked in the same manner. A light layer of batting is used underneath everything but the stems. Tiny invisible overcast stitches hold all these pieces in place.

The batting is a very thin layer of cotton. Each shape is outline quilted and the background is filled with ¾″ diamonds.

The color scheme is beige, green and rose on a white background. The beige is not figured; the green is a tiny print, and most of the rose color is actually a tiny, tiny red and white stripe. The blocks are identical except that the very middle one has a yellow center! It's almost impossible not to have a personal theory about a quilt. It looks as if this were a bridal quilt, and the yellow center was the "planned mistake" that insured good fortune.

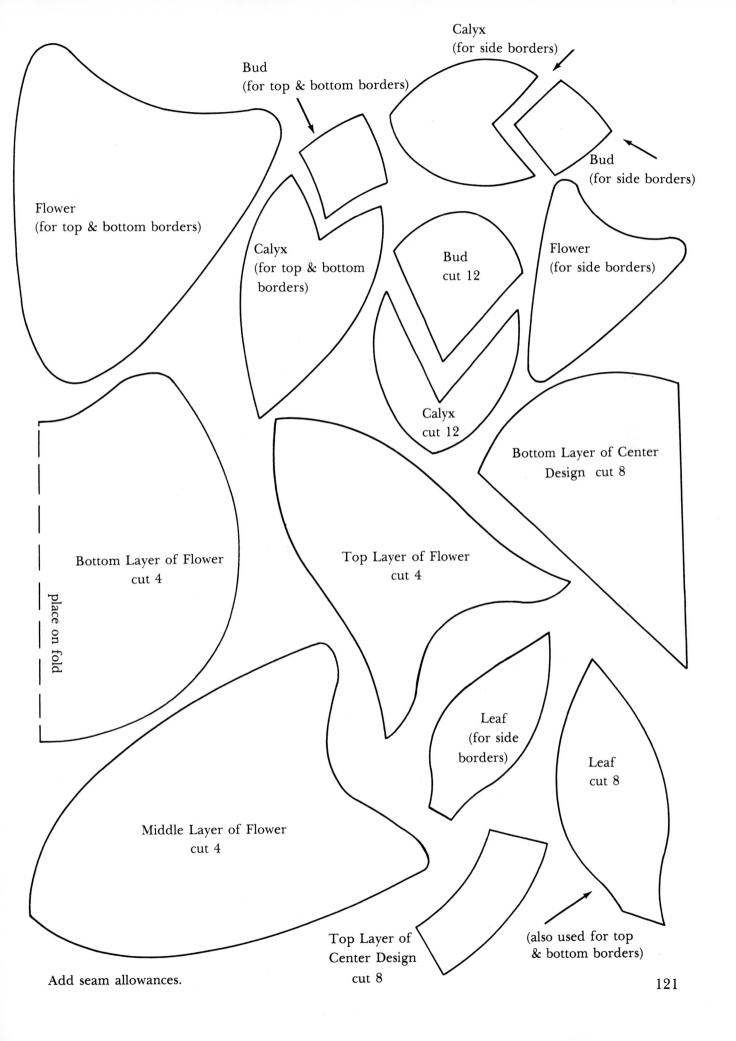

Flower
(for top & bottom borders)

Bud
(for top & bottom borders)

Calyx
(for side borders)

Bud
(for side borders)

Calyx
(for top & bottom borders)

Bud
cut 12

Flower
(for side borders)

Calyx
cut 12

Bottom Layer of Center
Design cut 8

place on fold

Bottom Layer of Flower
cut 4

Top Layer of Flower
cut 4

Leaf
(for side borders)

Leaf
cut 8

Middle Layer of Flower
cut 4

Top Layer of
Center Design
cut 8

(also used for top
& bottom borders)

Add seam allowances.

121

Morning Glory

(Photograph on page 53.)

From the collection of Robert and Helen Cargo; Tuscaloosa, Alabama.
Provenance of quilt: Tuscaloosa, Alabama; 1940.

Measure for Measure *(finished sizes)*
Finished quilt: 85½" x 95½"
Blocks: 8" x 7½"
Borders: 2¾" wide all around. Corners are not mitered.
Backing and binding: Cut in one piece. Backing comes to front to form a ⅜" binding.

This bold little flower shows its lovely face in the early mornings of late summer. In its natural state, it peeps out of roadside ditches and over old fences, but if you want to domesticate it, it will obligingly climb a trellis. A pure clear blue is perhaps the most familiar color of the morning glory, but sometimes you'll find it has pink and lavender blooms on the same vine! This quiltmaker didn't pick a favorite color; she included all three.

The pieced blocks are placed so that the flowers of one color climb the quilt diagonally, as if climbing from earth towards the heavens. The overall impression, though, is of a mass of various colored blooms. This is possible since sashing between blocks has been omitted.

This deceptively simple looking flower pattern actually has 12 pieces in each block. The blocks are relatively small, only 8" x 7½", so it takes 120 of them to make a quilt this size. Of course, this is a big quilt. You could make it smaller by dropping one row of blocks, and you would still have a good-size quilt. The little block is also appropriate for many other uses—for example, it would make a wonderful pocket or bib on a gardener's apron.

Another complexity of this quilt is seen in the placement of the fabric colors and prints. A print fabric is used for the inside of the blossom's trumpet, and although three different prints are involved, all the blue flowers have the same blue print; all the lavender flowers have the same lavender print, and all the pink flowers have the same pink print. There are three different greens in the quilt, two in the leaves and a third in the binding

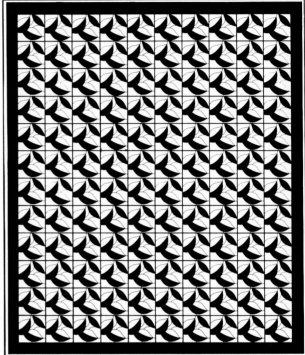

and backing. The white fabric is a plain muslin. It is very doubtful that it was pre-shrunk because there is some puckering in those portions of the quilt where the muslin was used. The puckering is not unpleasant; in fact, it adds an interesting texture to the quilt (a fortuitous happenstance; however, not to be counted on).

The quilting stitches are beautifully small and even. The quilting follows every seam, making an outline of each flower shape on the wrong side of the quilt. The backing of the quilt is green fabric. Those quilted flower shapes show up so perfectly on the green fabric that this quilt is actually reversible — as beautiful on one side as the other.

A simple 2¾"-wide border of the same fabric as the backing is quilted with a row of stitches right down the center. The backing was cut ½" larger all around to provide a binding for the outer edges of the quilt.

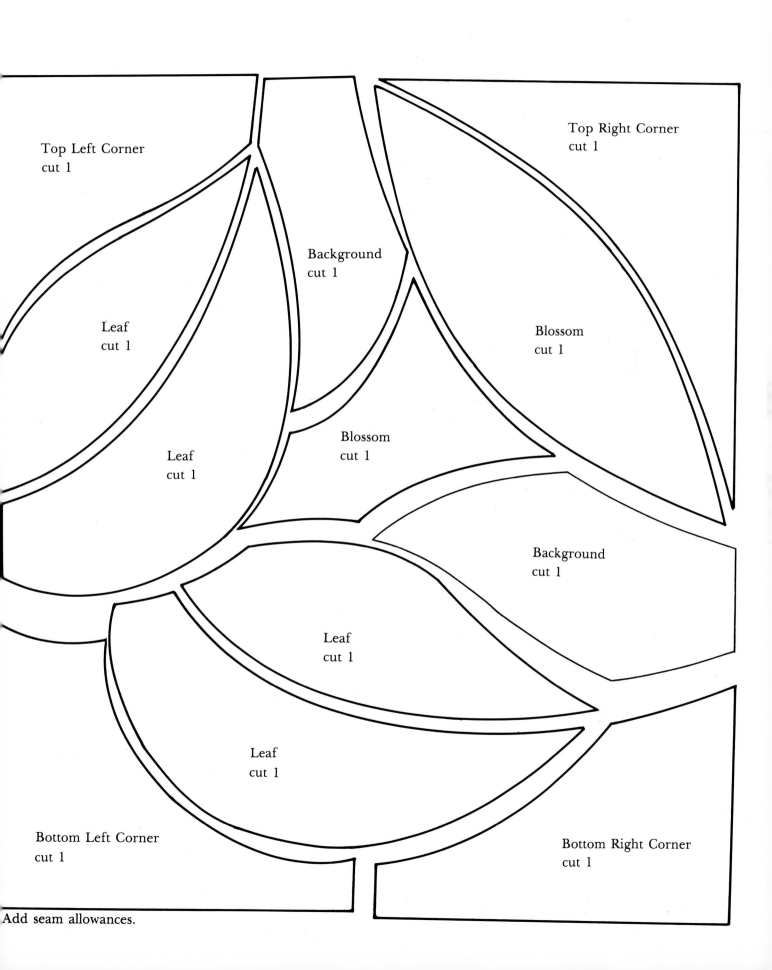

Top Left Corner
cut 1

Top Right Corner
cut 1

Background
cut 1

Leaf
cut 1

Blossom
cut 1

Leaf
cut 1

Blossom
cut 1

Leaf
cut 1

Background
cut 1

Leaf
cut 1

Leaf
cut 1

Bottom Left Corner
cut 1

Bottom Right Corner
cut 1

Add seam allowances.

Cherokee Rose

(Photograph on page 53.)

Designed, made, and owned by Anita Westerfield; Athens, Georgia; 1976.

Measure for Measure *(finished sizes)*
Finished quilt: 75″ x 103″
Blocks: 18″ x 18″
Borders: 15″ wide
Batting: Polyester
Backing: White percale
Binding: ½″

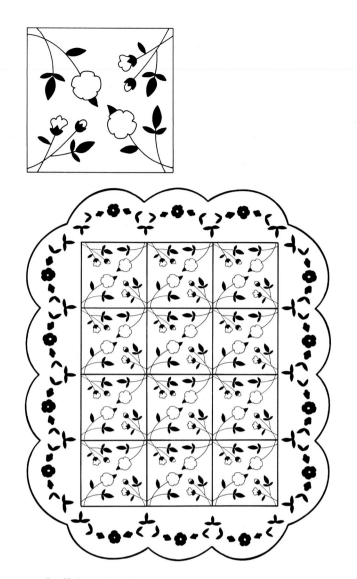

This is, quite simply, one of the most beautiful quilts we've ever seen. Mrs. Westerfield sent a block of this quilt into the *Progressive Farmer* quilt block contest in 1976, and the quilt eventually was published in a paperback book, *Country Quilt Patterns*. We think it deserves an encore, so we've included it in this collection of flower quilts.

Mrs. Westerfield made the quilt to commemorate that lovely, wild climbing rose which, she insists, is always white with a yellow center. She admits to seeing a pink rose similar to this when growing up in Kentucky, but "it was simply a wild rose—not a true Cherokee rose." The Cherokee rose has only one layer of petals, a total of five per bloom, which surround a large yellow center. It also has thorns, which Mrs. Westerfield has represented with a combination of briar and outline stitches as she embroidered the stems. Her embroidery skill is seen again in the detailing at the centers and on the edges of the flower shapes. She used a stem stitch around the outer edges and a combination of satin stitch and French knots in the centers.

The color scheme is all white on a blue background. The leaves are not green and the centers are not yellow. They are both white. It is the color scheme that makes the quilt so beautiful. Reversing the colors on the scalloped border is particularly effective.

Quilting in the shape of large diamonds, filled with smaller diamonds, is used in the open areas of the design where the blocks are joined together. Mrs. Westerfield said she was aiming for a trellis effect with the diamond quilting. Outline quilting follows the shape of the flowers, leaves, and stems, culminating with a diamond within a diamond at the center of the block.

Although she has made several of these quilts and has tried out different color schemes, this is still Mrs. Westerfield's favorite. She doesn't tire of the pattern, although she "reckons" it takes her 500 hours to make this quilt for a double bed.

124

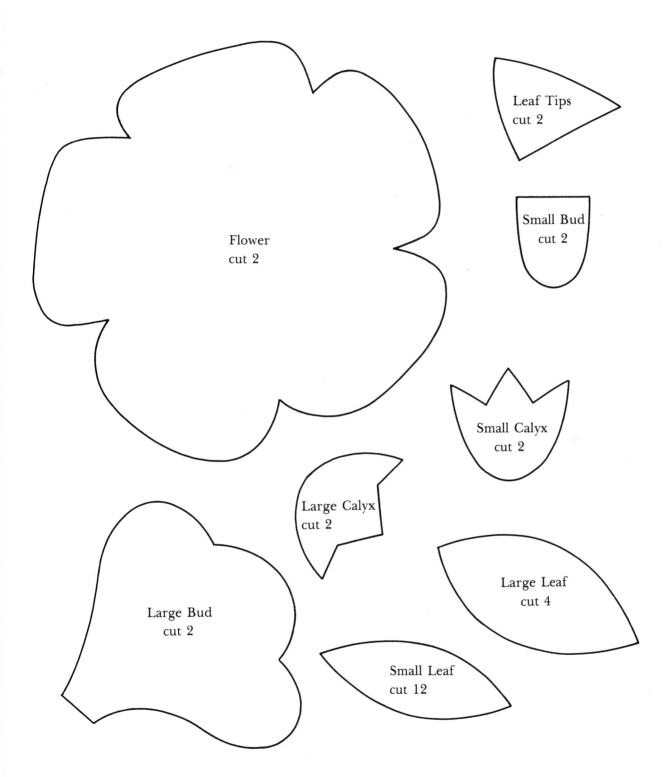

Flower
cut 2

Leaf Tips
cut 2

Small Bud
cut 2

Small Calyx
cut 2

Large Calyx
cut 2

Large Bud
cut 2

Large Leaf
cut 4

Small Leaf
cut 12

Add seam allowances.

Clematis

(Photograph on page 52.)

Designed, made and owned by Martha Skelton, Vicksburg, Mississippi; 1974.

Measure for Measure *(finished sizes)*
Finished quilt: 78½" x 87"
Flowered blocks: 8¼" square
Blue blocks: 8¼" square
White blocks: 8¼" square
Side triangles: 11¾" x 8¼" x 8¼"
Corner triangles: 8¼" x 6" x 6"
Green borders: 1" wide
White borders: 1½" wide
Green binding: ½" wide

How do you capture the airy lightness of a climbing flower? Martha Skelton does it by carefully selecting a number of blossom blocks and playing them against lots of white and sky blue. A trace of green hints at the vines and leaves which are necessary to support the plant, but the blossom itself is the dominant feature of this lovely quilt. Within each solid block, another bloom is quilted, making this truly a quilter's quilt!

A fine polyester and cotton blend is used for the solid fabric and white backing. Yellow straight stitches surround the puffy center of each flower, and a lighter green stem stitch traces the center of the two leaves.

All the seams that join blocks are quilted ¼" from each side of the seam, producing two rows of quilting ½" apart. The borders are outline quilted, as are the appliquéd flowers. Each petal is outlined, forming a secondary pattern over the leaves. The back side of the quilt looks like an all-white quilt with two types of flowers — the clematis flower and leaf in one block, the abstract four-petal in the next block. The ½"-wide channel of quilting around the block separates these two flowers. Since this is a Skelton quilt, of course the borders and binding are mitered. With all the detailed quilting and finishing work, this really is a reversible quilt, to be enjoyed equally on both sides.

126

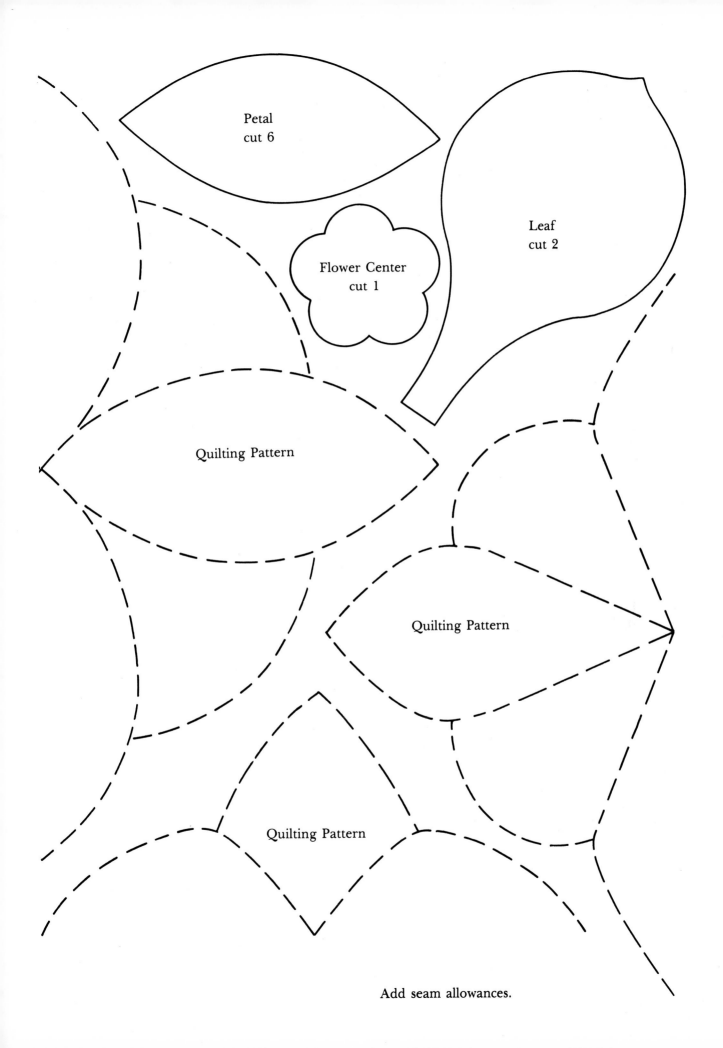

Petal
cut 6

Leaf
cut 2

Flower Center
cut 1

Quilting Pattern

Quilting Pattern

Quilting Pattern

Add seam allowances.

Tulip and Reel

(Photograph on page 54.)

From the collection of Robert and Helen Cargo; Tuscaloosa, Alabama.
Provenance of quilt: Pennsylvania; 1890.

Measure for Measure *(finished sizes)*
Finished quilt: 84½″ x 84½″
Patterned blocks: 15″ x 15″
Plain blocks: 15″ x 15″
Half blocks: 15″ x 15″ x 20½″
Quarter blocks: 10″ x 10″ x 15″
Borders: 10″ wide
Batting: Cotton
Backing: White cotton
Binding: ¼″ wide

One of the most popular early themes for quilt designs was a stylized flower or leaf used in partnership with a "reel." The "reel" must have been taken from the spool used to wind up the lines and ropes of sailing ships. It was interpreted here as a rectangular shape with elongated corners, surrounded by four crescents. An oak leaf, lily, tulip, or rose shape were the favorite accents for the corners of the rectangles.

The cockscomb in the border of this quilt was another favorite motif, evoking the early settlers' memories of Old England. The bristle shape of this motif is reminiscent of the plumes and decorations of military uniforms, but most of us know the cockscomb as a rigid little flower that dries well.

The red, yellow, and green color scheme has been a favorite of quilters since the 1830s because they were the most colorfast fabrics to be obtained. This quilt dates from 1890, so it is apparent that the maker took the motifs from one time period and the colors from a later period.

The motifs are appliquéd with tiny overcast stitches that are barely visible. This is a rather difficult pattern because of all the curves and points in the cockscomb.

The body of the work is quilted in feathered plumes which exactly fit in the triangles around the outer edge. The four white squares within the quilt are filled with two plumes that meet in the center—actually they are two of the triangles, placed face to face.

The patterned blocks are quilted in straight rows ½″ apart. Below the vine, the border is quilted in curved rows following the shape of the vine to the edge of the quilt. Above the vine, quilting forms a wave-like pattern, coming to a point in the center of each cockscomb. Notice the wonderful leafy stalk quilted at each corner of the quilt.

The backing is muslin, and of course, the batting is cotton. The binding is cut on the straight of grain, not on the bias, and is ¼″ wide on back and front.

There's a popular belief that the finer the quilting, the older the quilt. There may be older quilts than this, but there's hardly finer quilting!

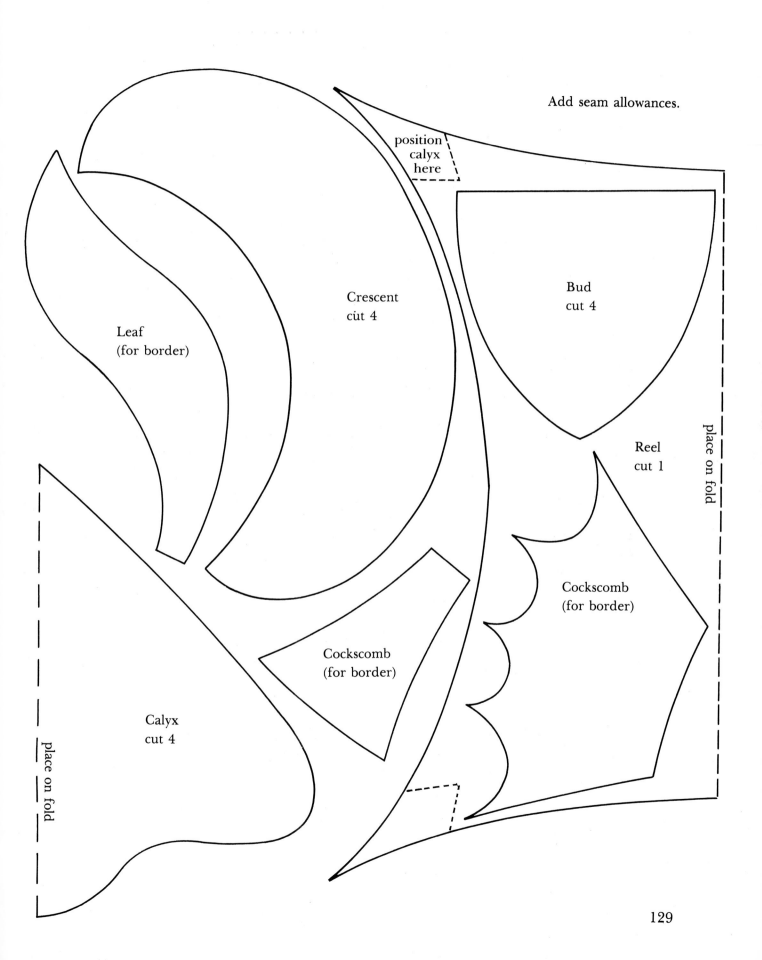

Add seam allowances.

position
calyx
here

Crescent
cut 4

Bud
cut 4

Leaf
(for border)

Reel
cut 1

Cockscomb
(for border)

Cockscomb
(for border)

place on fold

Calyx
cut 4

place on fold

129

Carolina Lily

(Photograph on page 55.)

Made and owned by Beulah Wilcox Wigley;
Robertsdale, Alabama; 1976.

 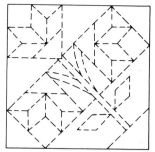

Measure for Measure *(finished sizes)*
Finished quilt: 77½" x 94½"
Patterned blocks: 8½" x 8½"
Plain blocks: 8½" x 8½"
Border: 7½" wide
Batting: Polyester
Binding: 1½" wide (cut backing and binding
 as one piece)

Of all the many ways this pattern can be
worked, this is surely one of the liveliest. The
bright, nodding heads of the lilies seem to be
just waiting for a spring breeze to come along
and scatter their petals across the quilt. Some-
how the meandering feather cable quilted into
the border makes us think of that breeze. And
in the bas-relief of the plain blocks we see a
hint of spring to come, of bulbs not yet
sprouted. All of these elements add up to a
quilt that is quite exciting, although it is
created from a familiar pattern.

Each block consists of three flowers pieced
with red petals and a green calyx. The stems
and leaves are appliquéd after the remainder
of the block has been sewn together. This
Carolina Lily ends in a bulb, but see "Grow
Your Own Flower Quilts" for other suggestions. The red and green fabrics are a polyester cotton blend, and the white fabric is
muslin.

Although the rows appear to be set on the
diagonal, they are really set in horizontal rows,
alternating patterned and plain blocks, and
are stair-stepped to get the diagonal look. The
need for half and quarter blocks is eliminated
when using this setting.

Since the backing of the quilt is solid red,
and it's quilted in white, every detail of that
perfect stitching stands out—another reversible quilt! Notice how the quilted diagonal
lines of the border form a chevron at the
center of each side.

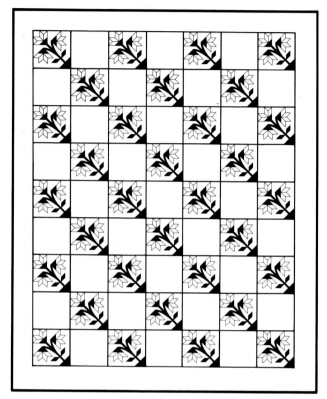

We asked Beulah Wigley when she made
this quilt, and she started figuring its age by
figuring the age of her children. "Let's see—I
gave that quilt to my son when he was forty.
No, he swapped it for the *Bear's Paw* when he
was forty. Let me see now. I quilted that quilt
in 1976, but I pieced it thirty years ago. You
know, that quilt has been used!" Beulah makes
all her quilts to be used, and they get to be
heirlooms only after they serve their time.

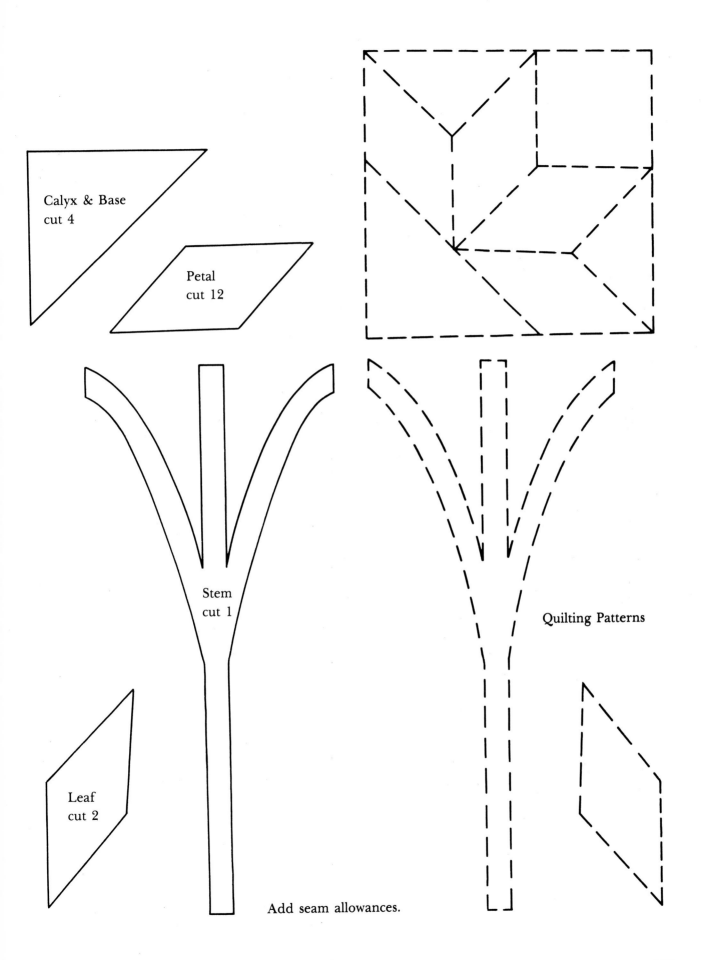

Calyx & Base
cut 4

Petal
cut 12

Stem
cut 1

Leaf
cut 2

Add seam allowances.

Quilting Patterns

131

Pomegranate

(Photograph on page 55.)

From the collection of the Museum of the City of Mobile; Mobile, Alabama.
Provenance of quilt: Mobile, Alabama; 1870.

Measure for Measure *(finished sizes)*

Finished quilt: 77″ x 89″

Block: 30″ x 30″

Sashing: 7″ wide, with 5 stripes sewn together as follows; a center stripe of 1″-wide green is bordered on each side by 1½″-wide stripes of orange and red. Center sashing is 67″ long; between blocks it is 30″ long.

Top border: 12″ wide with 7 stripes
Sew together the same as sashing, with the addition of another 1″ stripe of green and a 4″ stripe of red on the very outer edge.

Bottom border: 10″ wide, with 7 stripes
Sew together the same as the top border except outermost red stripe is only 2″ wide.

Side borders: 5″ wide with 4 stripes
Sew together from inside out as follows; 1½″-wide red, 1½″-wide orange, 1″-wide green, 1″-wide orange.

Binding: Cut an extra ½″ to fold to back on all outside edges.

This quilt was made by a young girl, approximately 16 or 17 years old, and then stored in her hope chest. She never used the quilt when she finished it because it was intended for use after she married and started housekeeping. It stayed in that hope chest until she was 60 years old, when she finally took it out and sold it to an antiques dealer. Several weeks later, the dealer happened to read that the woman had married. He offered to return the quilt, thinking that she would surely want it back, now that the occasion for which it had been made had finally occurred. He was hardly prepared for her answer.

"No, no, absolutely not. I wouldn't touch it with a ten foot pole! It kept me from getting married all these years, and I sure don't want it back now!"

The few facts we have about the quilt help us answer some of our questions. The age of the quiltmaker surely has something to do with the lack of expertise in her quilting; however, that same youthfulness accounts for the vibrant colorations of the sashing and borders. The difference in the sizes of the borders and their variation from the sashing may be explained in the fact that she was making it for a bed, as yet unseen, in a home not yet a reality.

Perhaps the quilter's age also had something to do with the backing of the quilt. It was made from grain sacks which had been cut open and pressed flat. Maybe her family was waiting to see how she "took to" quilting before they let her use new fabric.

The filling appears to be an old sheet or blanket. The quilting follows the lines of the motif within each square and outlines the stripes of the sashing and borders. Although the stitches aren't tiny, they are even, and the quilting pattern is graceful. It's too bad the young girl gave up quilting after this one effort.

132

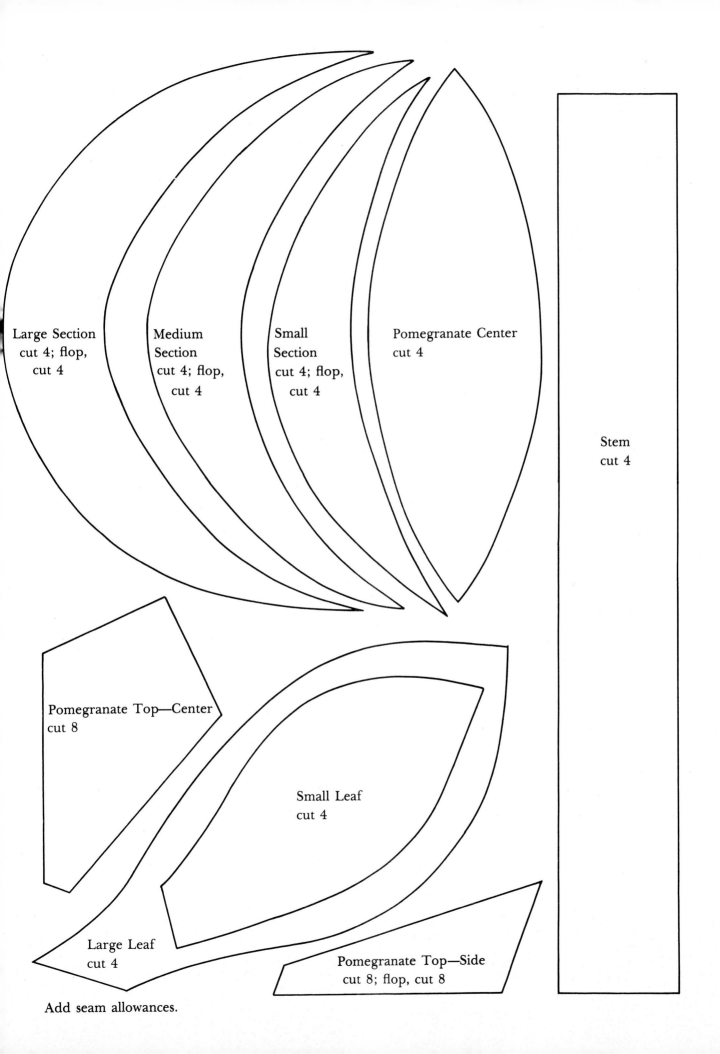

Large Section
cut 4; flop,
cut 4

Medium
Section
cut 4; flop,
cut 4

Small
Section
cut 4; flop,
cut 4

Pomegranate Center
cut 4

Stem
cut 4

Pomegranate Top—Center
cut 8

Small Leaf
cut 4

Large Leaf
cut 4

Pomegranate Top—Side
cut 8; flop, cut 8

Add seam allowances.

Colorado Remembrance

(Photograph on page 59.)

Designed, made, and owned by Martha Skelton; Vicksburg, Mississippi; 1982.

Measure for Measure
Finished Block: 22½″ square, with binding
White center square: 8¼″
Green band: 1″ wide
White band: ¾″ wide

A trip through the majestic Rocky Mountains was the inspiration for this little quilt block, which became a sort of "diary" of the two most memorable sights, the mountains and flowers. The coneflower (or brown-eyed Susan as it's often erroneously called) blooms prolifically in the mountain terrain.

The center appliqué of three little coneflowers is surrounded by a patchwork border of Rocky Mountains. An interlocking Chinese Puzzle border further enhances a simple block. The green band is pieced with a yellow 1″-square inset in each corner and attached to the 1⅞″-wide outer border. The white border may be appliquéd after the entire block is completed. Be sure and notice the mitered corners. The camel, brown, and green color scheme is a perfect choice to express the carefully chosen motifs. Outline quilting is used throughout the block with a detailing of little three-lobed flowers in the four large corner triangles.

The daisy-like appearance of this lovely wildflower often prompts that romantic test of "loves me, loves me not." Make sure your flower has an odd number of petals or start with "loves me not" to ensure you receive a positive response.

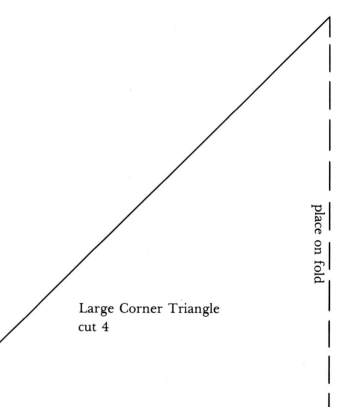

Large Corner Triangle
cut 4

place on fold

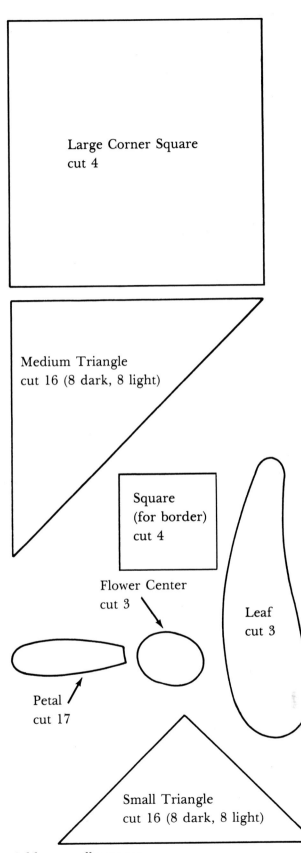

Large Corner Square
cut 4

Medium Triangle
cut 16 (8 dark, 8 light)

Square
(for border)
cut 4

Flower Center
cut 3

Leaf
cut 3

Petal
cut 17

Small Triangle
cut 16 (8 dark, 8 light)

Add seam allowances.

Marigold

(Photograph on page 56.)

Owned by Katherine Holmes; Gallion, Alabama.
Made by her great grandmother, Mrs. Castro Jane Harris Moore; Folsum, Alabama; 1850.

Measure for Measure *(finished sizes)*
Finished quilt: 71" x 85½"
Blocks: 14½" x 14½"
Sashing: 2¼"
Borders: 2¼"
Binding: ¼"
Backing: White muslin

This fresh little flower face could be that of several many-petaled flowers — marigold, sunflower, zinnia, dahlia. It features a large center circle ringed by two rows of petals, one of 12 red triangles, the other of 12 yellow diamonds. A row of 12 elongated shaped triangles finishes out the design to make a complete circle. The circle is set onto a background of white, and the blocks are sashed and bordered with green, and then bound in brown.

Mrs. Holmes feels very fortunate to have this quilt, as it has survived not one, but two different fires, and the worst damage it shows is some slight water stains. It and several other quilts have always been stored in a large chest, which has now twice saved them from fire.

The quilt is covered with close stitches. Each triangle and diamond is outlined quilted, and the stitching on each block repeats the shape of the square, decreasing in size until it reaches the flower. All of this intricate stitching creates a perfect reproduction of the pattern on the wrong side of the quilt.

The borders and sashing are stitched in concentric quarter circles with a thread that matches the color of the fabric. This little extra care shows that this quilt was special to the maker.

The batting, of course, is cotton, and Mrs. Holmes believes it was ginned locally. The cotton is of a fine quality, and there are no seeds in it. The Black Belt region of Alabama, the home of this quilt, was a leading producer of cotton before the War Between the States, so local quilters had access to high quality material for their fillers.

Pattern on next page.

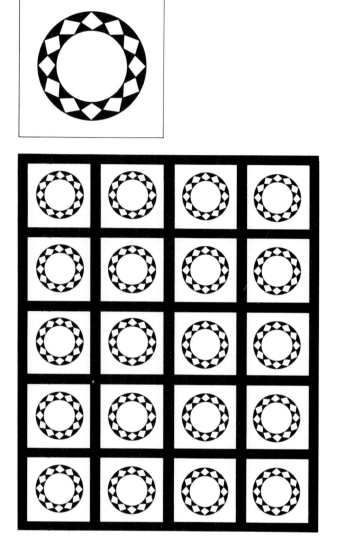

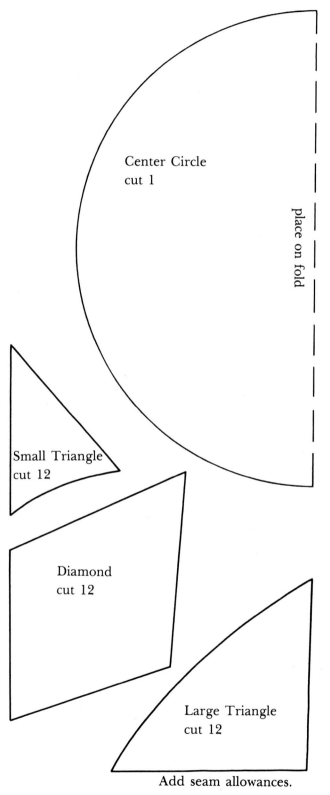

Center Circle
cut 1

place on fold

Small Triangle
cut 12

Diamond
cut 12

Large Triangle
cut 12

Add seam allowances.

The piecing of the square is not for a novice. Since there are so many points to be made, and the larger circle formed by the diamonds and triangles has to be perfectly round, this should not be a first quilt. Although none of this is easy, an experienced quilter will find the reward worth the effort, as this is one of the cheeriest quilts around.

Triple Sunflower

(Photograph on page 57.)

Owned by Imogene Moon Winsett; Hazel Green, Alabama.
Designed and made by Georgia Della Harris Moon Galligan; Pond Beat (Huntsville), Alabama; 1933.

Measure for Measure *(finished sizes)*
Finished quilt: Approximately 72" x 96"
Blocks: 17½" x 17½"
Half blocks: 17½" x 17½" x 24½"
Quarter blocks: 12½" x 12½" x 17½"
Binding: ½" wide
Backing: Muslin
Yardage requirements for 45"-wide fabric:

    Brown: ¾ yard
    Green: ¾ yard
    Gold: 3¾ yard
    White: 3 yards
    Backing fabric: 5½ yards

Sometimes sunflowers bear one gigantic blossom on a tall stalk; other varieties branch and bear many star-like blooms. Sometimes they stand watch in a garden; other times they run rampant down a fencerow or out across a field. But no matter when or where you see them, sunflowers always command a second look. They are majestic!

You may remember Mrs. Winsett's *Triple Tulip*—her *Triple Sunflower* is just as fine, and illustrates once again that a grouping of three flowers is very effective.

A naturalistic color scheme, worked in solid fabrics, is a good choice for this pattern. Although the white muslin background is very effective, a dark background would be even more dramatic.

To make a single sunflower block, cut an 8½"-square block from white fabric. Cut one center from brown fabric, eight petals from gold, and four triangles and four squares from the white muslin. There are 54 single sunflower blocks in all and 18 plain white blocks.

To make a triple sunflower block sew three single sunflower blocks and one plain white block together. Appliqué two leaves on a plain block and then appliqué bias-tape stems. Repeat for all 18 triple sunflower blocks.

To assemble your quilt, sew your blocks together on the diagonal. You will have two rows with one block, two rows with three blocks, and two rows with five blocks. Sew the half blocks and quarter blocks in position before sewing your rows together and completing the top.

Quilt spirals in each sunflower center; quilt just inside each pieced shape and around each appliquéd leaf and stem. Straight-line quilting is used in the half blocks, but you might try repeating the sunflower motif. If making an entire quilt seems to be an overwhelming undertaking, make a triple sunflower block for a pillow as shown in the photograph on page 62.

Pattern on next page.

Continuation of *Triple Sunflower.*

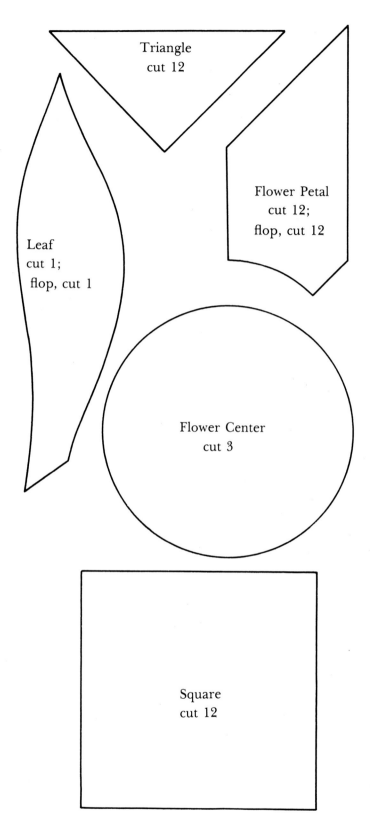

Triangle
cut 12

Flower Petal
cut 12;
flop, cut 12

Leaf
cut 1;
flop, cut 1

Flower Center
cut 3

Square
cut 12

Add seam allowances.

Sunflower Discs

(Photograph on page 58.)

Designed and made by Chris Wolf Edmonds; Lawrence, Kansas; 1979.

Measure for Measure *(finished sizes)*
Finished disc: 14″, including hoop

One state highway marker in the shape of a sunflower inspired Chris Edmonds to create these interpretations of the Kansas state flower. She knew she wanted to frame her finished designs in wooden embroidery hoops, so she kept the basic circular shape for all the variations. The flower itself suggested the petal arrangements. Chris used a compass and protractor to work out the designs for the petals, then put them together as she worked. Some are appliquéd onto the background of muslin. Others are pieced and then appliquéd in place.

Colors closely follow those of the real sunflower, ranging from rust to orange to bright yellow. The brown prints suggest the highly textured center of the flower, the mother lode of sunflower seeds! Well-chosen prints on the petals catch the effect of dappled sunshine.

For a delightful finishing detail, you can make the stems and hang your sunflower discs in a wall grouping. And, of course, you could certainly make a fabulous quilt by placing the flowers on squares instead of circles or by setting circles into a background of green sashing.

Each sunflower requires ½ yard of muslin in addition to fabric scraps of your choosing. Cut two muslin circles for each flower, one for the appliqué base and the other for the backing. Make templates for your selected pieces.

For patterns one, two, and three, trace the entire outline of the sunflower and appliqué that big solid piece to one of the muslin circles; then stitch the additional petals and centers into place. On patterns one and two, piece the small circle of diamonds and triangles and appliqué in place. Each piece is applied separately for pattern three.

For patterns four and five, piece all of the petal ring, then appliqué it in the center of the muslin circle.

Quilt the disc in the same 14″ hoop you plan to use for display, following the quilting lines on the pattern.

To finish, spring the outside hoop forward about ¹/₁₆″ and cut off excess batting and fabric with a razor blade, leaving a small flap of the top fabric at the hoop opening to fold under. Run a line of white glue along the edge of the fabric, push the hoop back together, and let the glue dry.

For each leaf, cut a front and back from green fabric and one leaf from quilt batting. Chris used two to four leaves for each of her stems. Place the fabric pieces right sides together with batting underneath. Stitch seams, leaving one side of the stem and the bottom of the leaf open for turning. Turn right side out and quilt as indicated by the broken lines on the pattern. Make a small loop in one end of a 13″ length of florist wire. Insert the loop end through the stem up to the tip of the leaf and gently bend the wire to shape and support the leaf.

To make stems, use a 35″, 40″, or 50″ dowel. Cut a length of fabric 5″ longer than dowel and wide enough to go around it, adding a ⅝″ seam allowance on each edge. Lay the fabric strip along the length of the dowel and make ¼″ slits in the fabric where the leaves are to be placed (5″ to 6″ apart). Insert the leaf stems through the slits and fasten to the dowel by wrapping tape around the ends of the florist wire and the dowel. Stitch the sides and bottom edge of the strip around dowel closed. The remainder of the fabric strip will extend 2½″ to 3″ above the top edge of the dowel. Turn this under ½″, stitch and then tack this to the quilting hoop.

Chris thinks the variations for these flowers are almost endless. Why not see if you can add to these?

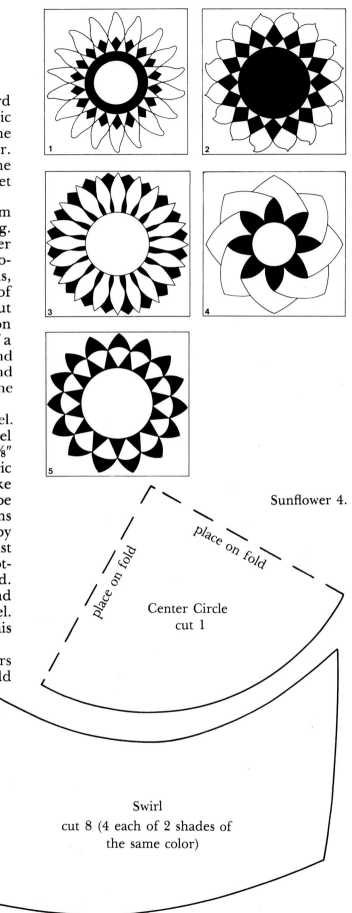

Sunflower 4.

place on fold

place on fold

Center Circle
cut 1

Petal
cut 8

Swirl
cut 8 (4 each of 2 shades of
the same color)

Add seam allowances.

Pattern continued on next page.

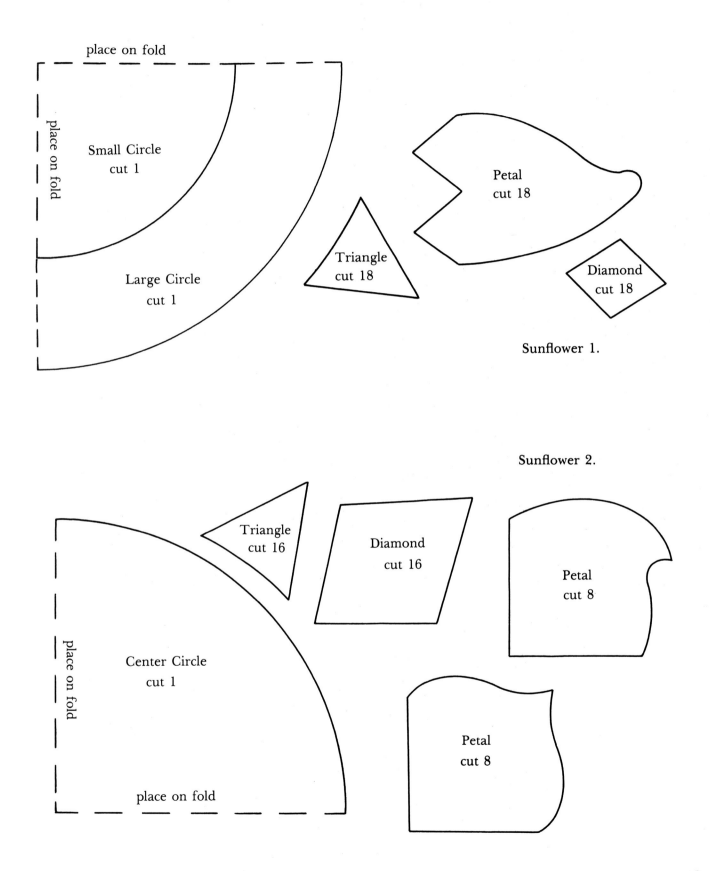

place on fold

place on fold

Small Circle
cut 1

Large Circle
cut 1

Triangle
cut 18

Petal
cut 18

Diamond
cut 18

Sunflower 1.

Sunflower 2.

Triangle
cut 16

Diamond
cut 16

Petal
cut 8

place on fold

Center Circle
cut 1

Petal
cut 8

place on fold

Add seam allowances.

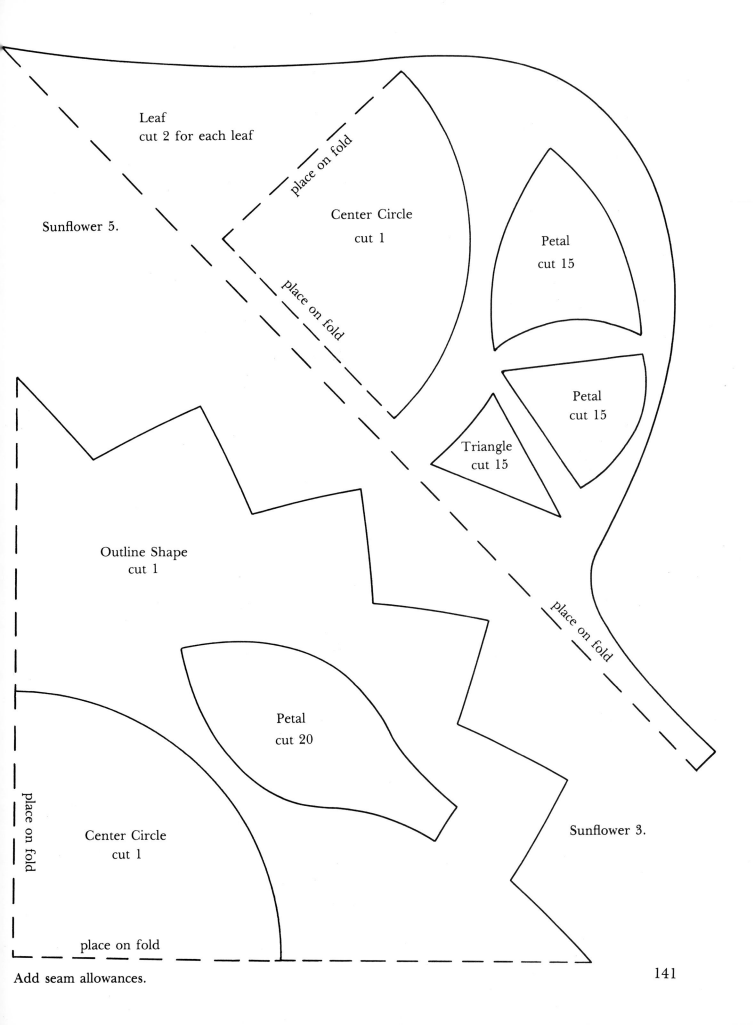

Leaf
cut 2 for each leaf

place on fold

place on fold

Sunflower 5.

Center Circle
cut 1

Petal
cut 15

Petal
cut 15

Triangle
cut 15

Outline Shape
cut 1

place on fold

Petal
cut 20

Sunflower 3.

place on fold

Center Circle
cut 1

place on fold

Add seam allowances.

141

Calico Wreath

(Photograph on page 60.)

Designed, made and owned by Ann Fentress; Mobile, Alabama; 1983.

Measure for Measure *(finished sizes)*
Finished quilt: 18″ x 86″
Center block with wreath: 18″ x 32″
Bordered star block: 18″ x 18″
Flying geese border: 18″ x 6″
Outer peach border: 3″
Binding: ½″ all around

What a perfect solution for a sideboard or table! Your centerpiece is stitched right onto your table cover. The elongated oval of the center wreath seems to be just waiting for a big platter of holiday goodies, as the star blocks add their own twinkle.

A superb selection of fabrics results in a well coordinated color scheme for today's contemporary homes. The warm peach and darker russet are complemented by a very dark, almost black, green color. The prints are well-chosen, especially the small floral pattern with the white background. It provides enough textural interest to set it apart from the muslin fabric, and yet the pattern is still delicate enough to take a secondary position to the other strong prints and colors. This example proves the point that everything can't dominate if you want a good design. Some parts have to overshadow others to accomplish a sense of balance. Ann has mastered this lesson with the help of a very special teacher, her mother, Martha Skelton. You can see several examples of Martha's own work throughout the book.

Ann took the familiar *President's Wreath* and lengthened it to get the oval shape she needed to fit the space. Notice how she worked in extra leaves on the outside of the oval. She appliquéd her flowers in place with a little polyester batting underneath each to keep them puffy. Patchwork was chosen for the borders, the star block and the strip of flying geese.

Outline quilting is used throughout the piece, with an extra row worked where necessary. The background of the wreath is filled with 1″ diamonds. The backing is muslin, and the batting is polyester. Because it's in constant use by an active family, it was planned to be completely washable and had been washed many times before we took this photograph.

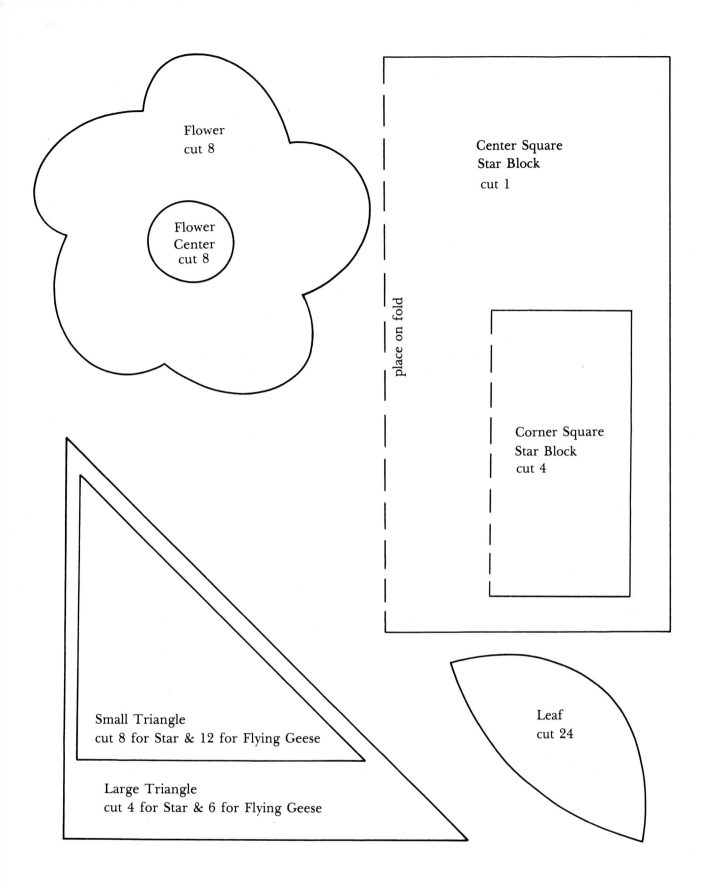

Flower
cut 8

Flower
Center
cut 8

Center Square
Star Block

cut 1

place on fold

Corner Square
Star Block
cut 4

Small Triangle
cut 8 for Star & 12 for Flying Geese

Large Triangle
cut 4 for Star & 6 for Flying Geese

Leaf
cut 24

Add seam allowances.

Poinsettia

(Photograph on page 61.)

From the collection of Robert and Helen Cargo; Tuscaloosa, Alabama.
Provenance of quilt: Dallas County, Alabama; 1920.

Measure for Measure *(finished sizes)*
Finished quilt: 72″ x 83″
Motif: Approximately 30″ x 30″
Binding: ½″
Batting: Cotton
Backing: White broadcloth

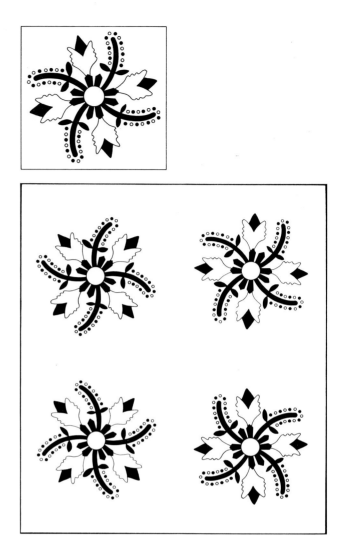

When you look at this quilt, you know immediately that the flower is a poinsettia. Yet, when you analyze the features of the design, none of them are very much like a poinsettia at all. A big center circle overlaps eight small petals, from which burst enormous bud-like shapes. Wild stems, each bearing 14 berries in two colors, twirl either clockwise or counterclockwise—the direction alternates in each of the four motifs. In spite of all this activity, an overall harmony is achieved, and the resulting quilt is a gay herald of the holiday season. Its charm lasts far beyond Christmas; the lively folk-art quality it conveys makes it a candidate for a year-round accessory.

The colors used to execute this unique design are extremely well chosen, and that is the reason it holds together. A realistic color scheme of red, gold, and dark green makes the flowers easily recognizable.

At first glance, it looks as though this quilt is made from four 36″-square blocks. Closer investigation, however, reveals that both the top and the back are pieced down the center. Two 36″ pieces are sewn together with a very narrow seam, creating a top almost 72″ in width and 83″ in length.

The four poinsettias are appliquéd to the white background fabric, working from the outside of the motif toward the center. The red "buds" go down first, then the green sheathing surrounding the bud, and finally the red petal near the center of the flower. Next, the twirling stems (cut from bias to equal a finished width of ¾″) and the leaves are added. The last pieces to be appliquéd are the flower center and the berries.

The berries are not stuffed, thank goodness. They're so uncomfortable to the touch when they're stuffed!

The quilting repeats the appliqué design in its entirety at the center of the quilt. Three buds and the center flower are used at the middle of each side of the quilt. The corners incorporate two buds and the whole flower. The appliquéd flowers are outline quilted. If there was a vacant space after all this quilting, the maker filled that space with concentric circles. Her quilting is very fine, and the back of the quilt is quite pleasing.

It seems that the best way to make this quilt would be to mark the background fabric with the location of the appliqués, stitch them in place, and then mark the quilting so that it fits nicely between the flowers.

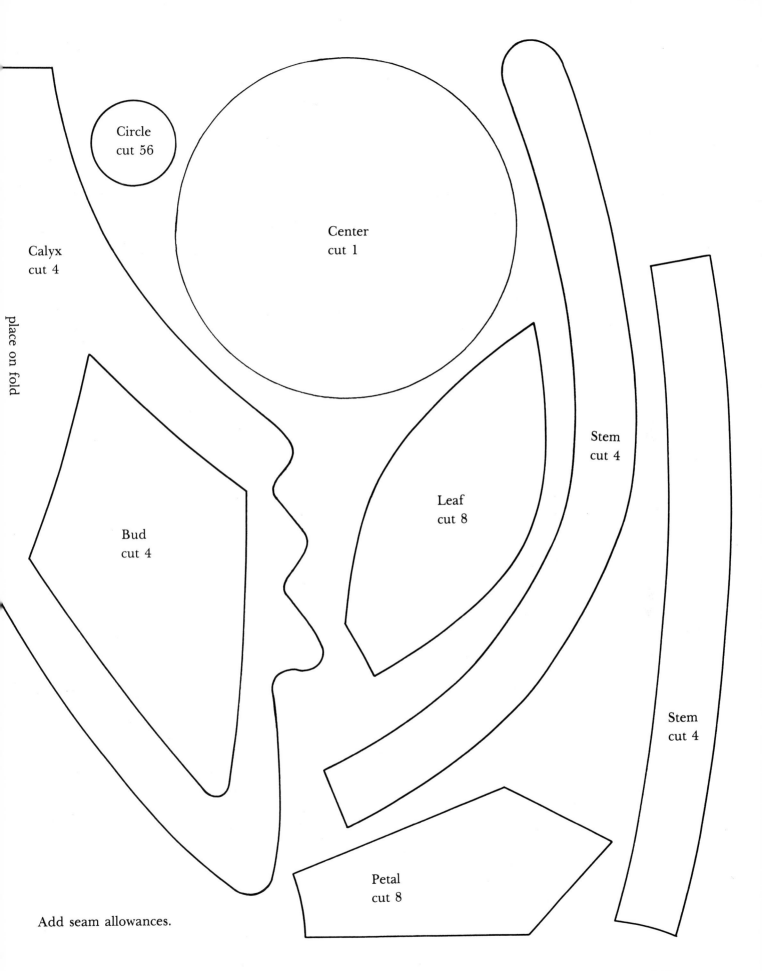

Circle
cut 56

Center
cut 1

Calyx
cut 4

place on fold

Stem
cut 4

Bud
cut 4

Leaf
cut 8

Stem
cut 4

Petal
cut 8

Add seam allowances.

145

Princess Feather

(Photograph on page 61.)

From the collection of Robert and Helen Cargo; Tuscaloosa, Alabama.
Provenance: Northport, Alabama; 1920.

Measure for Measure *(finished sizes)*

Finished quilt: 85″ x 90″

Blocks: 25½″ x 25½″

Top borders: Green; 1¾″ x 85″
 Gold; 4″ x 25½″
 Red; 3¾″ square

Bottom borders: Green; 1¼″ x 85″
 Gold; 4″ x 25½″

Border blocks: 3¾″, same design as corner
 block in sashing (see pattern)

There are no side borders.

Batting: Cotton

Backing: Muslin

Binding: ¼″-wide muslin

The alternating colors in the petals of this *Princess Feather* produce a lively effect of a whirling windmill. That feeling, combined with wonderful red and gold colors, makes this a cheerful addition to any room, especially at holiday time. You couldn't find a better quilt to carry through a warm country feeling for your Thanksgiving, Christmas, or New Year's decorating. There is a primitive quality to the design which makes the quilt an attractive companion for oak baskets, decoys, weathervanes, and other "country" pieces.

The original color scheme was red, gold, and green, but fortuitous fading has changed the green to a perfectly acceptable brown. Traces of the original green are still visible in tiny areas of the sashing. The fading of the green arouses curiosity because colorfast fabrics had been perfected by the time this quilt was made. Perhaps the fabric was home-dyed, or maybe the quilter used an older piece. It's fun to speculate.

This is the only machine appliquéd piece in the book, and it is included because it is approximately 65 years old. Short machine stitches placed precisely on the edges of each shape, matching thread colors, and edges turned smoothly under, even on the curves, are all examples of the very careful workman-ship exhibited here. We have a tendency to think of machine appliqué as a means of getting a job done quickly, but this woman obviously chose what she felt was the best technique, and maybe she wanted to flaunt her skill with the machine! So the machine was by no means used as a shortcut method here—it was the preferred method.

Care with detail is evident throughout the quilt. The quilting was done by hand, in scallops; the stitching is grouped in rows of three, spaced about 1″ apart. This gives an unusual touch to a fairly common quilting design often used on "work" quilts.

Two colors were chosen for the sashing and borders, which were also carefully planned. The borders are slightly different from each other on top and bottom because of the fabric, and they are completely different from the sashing. An extra effort was taken to make corner blocks that are intricately pieced.

146

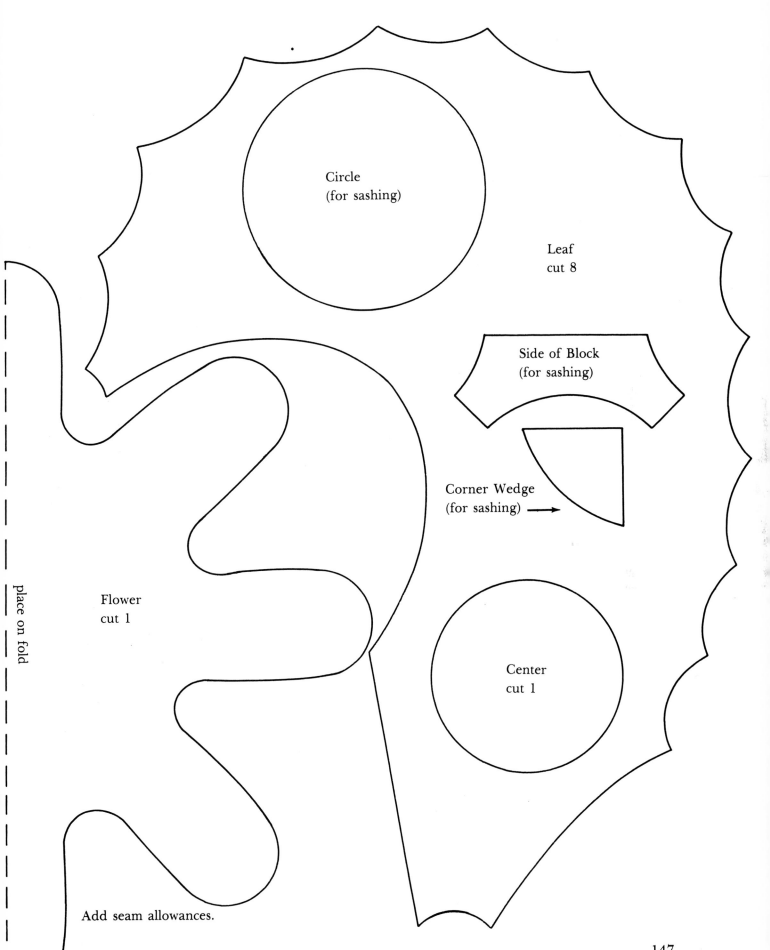

Circle
(for sashing)

Leaf
cut 8

Side of Block
(for sashing)

Corner Wedge
(for sashing) ⟶

place on fold

Flower
cut 1

Center
cut 1

Add seam allowances.

Winter Tulip

(Photograph on page 4.)

Owned by Jeannette Norman Middleton; Greenville, Alabama.
Made by her paternal grandmother, Mary Elizabeth Sheppard Norman; Fort Deposit, Alabama; 1870.

Measure for Measure *(finished sizes)*

Finished quilt: 73½" x 96"

Blocks: 20" x 20"

Side borders: 2½" x 89"

Top and bottom borders: 3" x 67½"

Corner blocks: 3" x 2½"

Sashing: 2½" x 20"

Corner blocks of sashing: 2½" x 2½"

Binding: ½" wide

   Round off outside corner when applying binding.

Backing: Unbleached muslin

Batting: Cotton

All sizes are approximate because quilt is very old and out of square.

We call this *Winter Tulip* because the original reds in this quilt have faded to a nice camel color, producing a very contemporary color scheme.

Our example of this popular old pattern comes from Greenville, Alabama. I have seen three other quilts almost exactly like it within a 100-mile radius of Greenville. It leads one to speculate that the quilt pattern appeared in a popular publication of the time and everybody made it exactly as it was shown in the publication; or the four women who made the quilts knew and corresponded with each other, trading snippets of fabric and patterns.

If you keep an eye out for old quilts, you will see this pattern many times. It was often sewn in red and yellow, or in red and green with a print used for the center panel. The blocks were almost always made in exactly the same fabrics. No hodgepodge of prints or colors for this pattern!

The original pattern is pieced, forming approximately a 20" square; however, for ease in construction we have given the pieces to appliqué. The stems are appliquéd with a running stitch. All the work in this quilt is done by hand, and it would be almost impossible to achieve the curves otherwise, especially on the chevron-shaped pieces that meet at the center.

Outline quilting is used throughout, except on the sashing and borders, where diagonal stripes are stitched ½" apart.

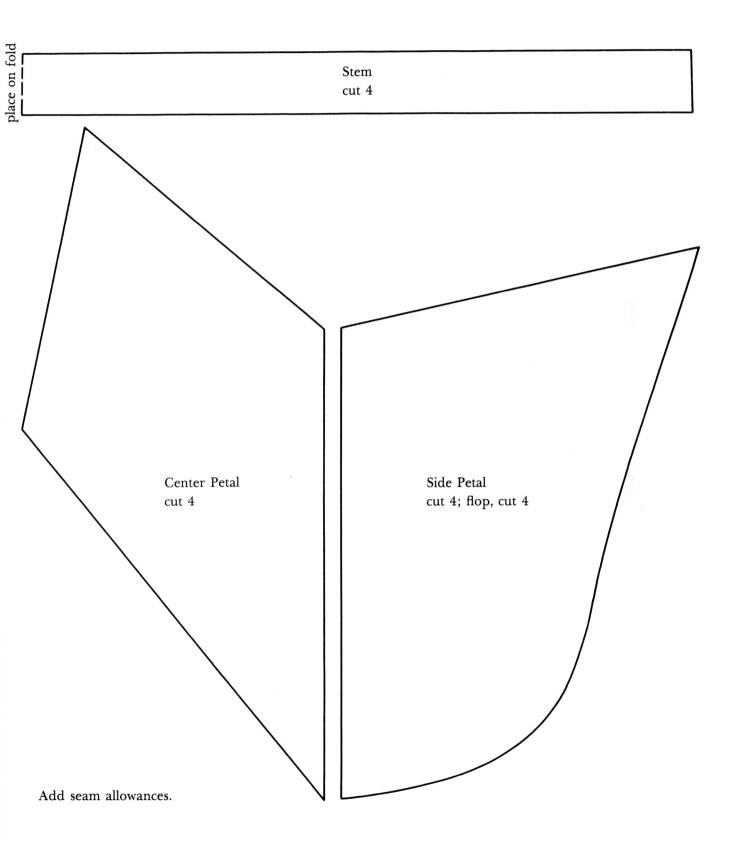

place on fold

Stem
cut 4

Center Petal
cut 4

Side Petal
cut 4; flop, cut 4

Add seam allowances.

149

Tulip Cross

(Photograph on page 8.)

From the collection of Dick and Marti Michell; Atlanta, Georgia.
Provenance: Pennsylvania; 1865.

Measure for Measure *(finished sizes)*

Finished quilt: 84″ x 84″
Blocks: 33″ square
Motifs: Approximately 31″ square
Stripe borders: Each 1″ wide
Outer border: Approximately 6″ wide
Batting: Lightweight cotton

When this collector attended a quilt auction, she thought she was bidding on a quilt of Amish bars. Imagine her surprise when she took possession of the quilt, and found this delightful pattern on the other side. Folklore has it that the village elder in the Amish or Mennonite communities dictated what designs could be used for quilt tops. In this case, he decreed that a pattern of bars was to be used on the front of the quilt; he never thought to specify what was to go on the back. So, this quiltmaker chose a pattern that was very popular at that time, the *Tulip Cross* or *Tulip and Princess Feather.* She has also added an eight-petaled daisy at the center of her design. This personal expression reveals a lively sense of color and movement, very similar in spirit to *Spider Lily,* which probably was produced under the same religious restrictions as this quilt. When considering this cultural climate, we can only marvel at such expressions of individuality, and wonder how many talented needle artists never found the courage to express themselves as boldly as these two quiltmakers (see Recommended Reading for more about the Amish and their quilts).

The stripes on the quilt "top" are all the same width, about 5½″. The quilt is bordered on all four sides with red. The colors, although a little peculiar on their own, work extremely well together. The gold is a muddy mustard color, and the green is off-color, but combined with the deep red, they make a wonderfully harmonious scheme.

On the patterned side of the quilt, the mustard color is a perfect background for the red blossoms and green foliage. The tulip shape is complemented by the little roses (very much like the roses in *Spider Lily),* and the daisy at the center of all this is without parallel!

The construction of the quilt is all done by hand, including the piecing of the striped side. The daisies and tulips are pieced, and they and the other shapes are appliquéd with tiny hand stitches. The center of the rose is reverse appliqué.

The inner border of the three stripes provides a nice frame for the four lively motifs. They are balanced with a mustard-colored border which is turned to the striped side of the quilt and used as the binding.

Quilting follows the shape of the appliqué pieces. Two rows about ⅛″ apart are used around each edge. One row is stitched on the edge of the appliquéd piece, and the other row is just off the edge. The background is filled with ½″ diamonds, and the border is quilted with a cable, six rows of stitches forming each side. Three rows of quilting run the length of each feather.

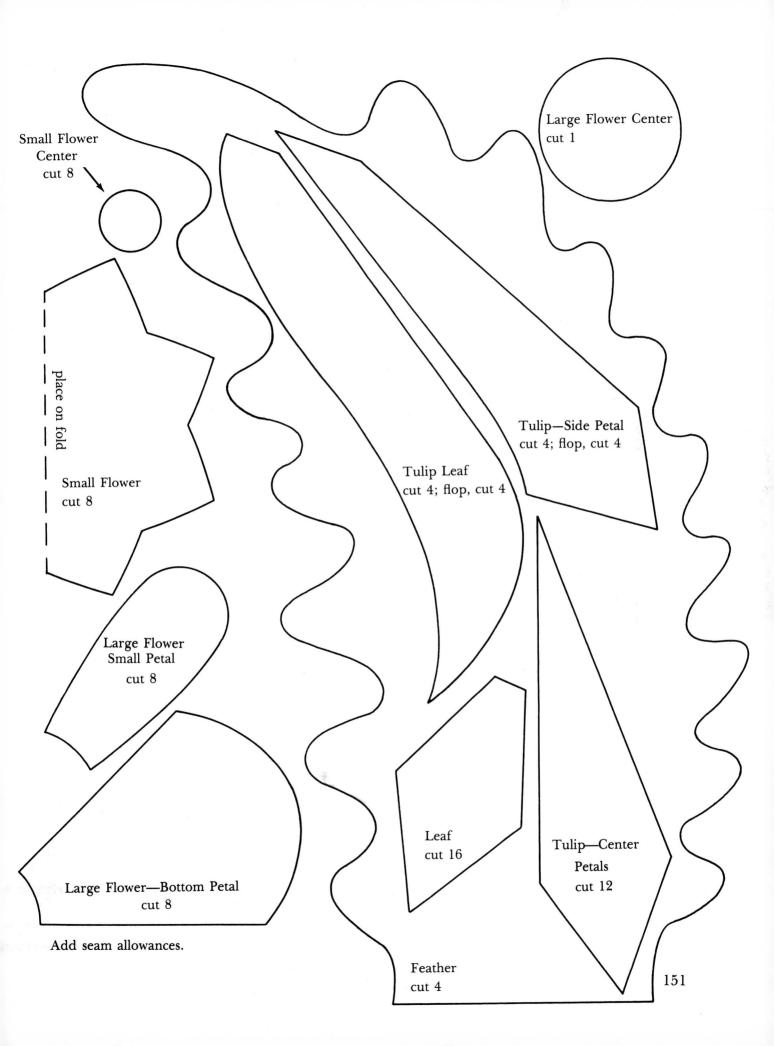

Small Flower
Center
cut 8

Large Flower Center
cut 1

place on fold

Small Flower
cut 8

Tulip Leaf
cut 4; flop, cut 4

Tulip—Side Petal
cut 4; flop, cut 4

Large Flower
Small Petal
cut 8

Leaf
cut 16

Tulip—Center
Petals
cut 12

Large Flower—Bottom Petal
cut 8

Add seam allowances.

Feather
cut 4

151

Spider Lily

(Photograph on page 9.)

From the collection of Rick and Mary Grunbaum; Dallas, Texas.
Provenance: Pennsylvania; 1880.

Measure for Measure *(finished sizes)*
Finished quilt: 88½" x 88½"
Spider lily motifs: Approximately 22½" square
Bouquet motifs: Approximately 22½" square
Zigzag border: 2½" wide
Solid blue border: 7" wide

Bright reds and yellows dance across a blue background, and the streak-of-lightning zig-zag border adds even more zing to this exuberant quilt.

If you look into a spider lily blossom, you will see that the flower is made of many tiny blooms radiating from a center. This eight-pointed shape is made by folding a 22½" square in half, folding the half in half, folding the small square in half *diagonally*, and then folding one side of the right angle to the long side of the triangle. Position the pattern against the folds.

The second motif is a bouquet of roses and tulips, anchored in the center by a four-pronged shape similar in feeling to the spider lily. This shape can also be made by folding your square in half on the diagonal, and in half again, and once again (3 folds). Trace your template with edges against the folds of the fabric. The bold red of these two dominant shapes adds emphasis to the negative areas formed by the parts of the red that have been cut away. The blue print background fabric provides the necessary contrast for the motifs. The quilt is not worked in blocks; the nine motifs are placed on a 69½" background square, with a bouquet motif in the center and in each corner; the spider lily centers each side. The work is meticulous in the appliqué and the reverse appliqué used for the centers of the roses and the yellow diamonds.

The zigzag border is actually a series of red and yellow triangles placed with the bases of the yellow triangles together.

Each shape, including zigzags, is stitched on both sides of the seam or edge so that the lines are a scant ¼" apart, which gives a very nice effect on the reverse side. Hex symbols of a flower within a circle are stitched into the centers of the spider lilies and into the spaces between the motifs, including the corners. The wide blue border is quilted with a cable pattern, with six rows of stitching forming each side of the cable. The background of the quilt is filled with 2" diamonds.

The other side of the quilt is a version of a machine-stitched Amish bar design. A 3½" red bar is in the exact center, and the bars to either side measure 3½", 7¼", 7¼", 3½", 3½", 3½", 7", 7" in width. The colors of the 17 bars are arranged the same on either side of the center. The colors are: red center, black print, pink print, black print, pink print, blue (from the other side), pink print, black print, pink print. There is no binding, and there doesn't appear to be any batting. The edges have been turned to the inside and held in place with a running stitch (see *Tulip Cross* for more about Amish bars).

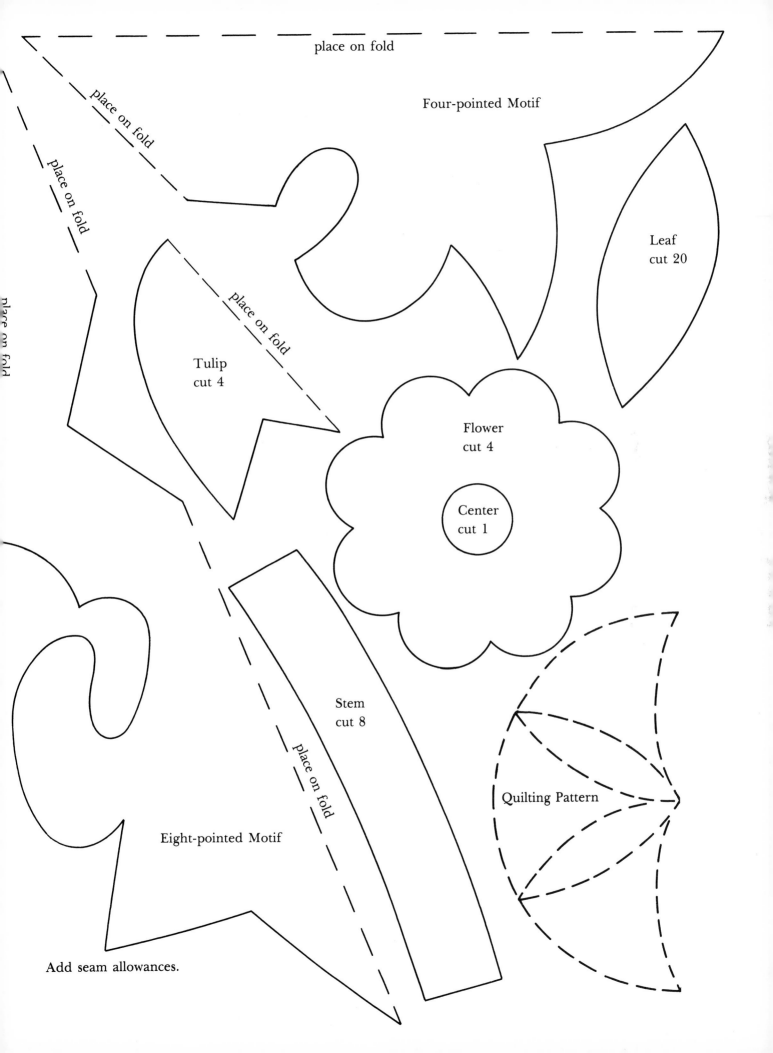

place on fold

Four-pointed Motif

place on fold

place on fold

Leaf
cut 20

place on fold

place on fold

place on fold

Tulip
cut 4

Flower
cut 4

Center
cut 1

Stem
cut 8

Eight-pointed Motif

place on fold

Quilting Pattern

Add seam allowances.

Recommended Reading

For ideas, information, and input about flowers, try the following books. All are beautifully illustrated, and many offer interesting tales of flower lore, as well as fascinating information.

The Scented Garden by Rosemary Verey, Van Nostrand Reinhold, 1981.

In and Out of the Garden by Sara Midda, Workman, 1981.

Plant and Floral Woodcuts for Designers & Craftsmen, selected and arranged by Theodore Menten, Dover, 1974.

The Old-Fashioned Cutting Garden, by Jack Kramer, drawings by Judifer Yellich, Macmillan, 1979.

Living with the Flowers by Denise Diamond, illustrated by Patricia Waters, William Morrow & Co., Inc. 1982.

Wildflowers in Color by Arthur Stupka, Harper Colophon Books, Harper & Row, 1965.

The Audubon Society Field Guide to North American Wildflowers by William A. Niering and Nancy Olmstead, Knopf, 1979.

The Color Dictionary of Flowers and Plants, by Roy Hay and Patrick M. Synge, The Royal Horticultural Society, and Crown, 1969.

To learn more about quilts, their history and traditions, and the women who shaped the heritage we now enjoy, look to the following.

Quilts in America by Patsy and Myron Orlofsky, McGraw-Hill, 1974. Required reading for anyone seriously interested in quilts.

Needlework in America by Virginia Churchill Bath, Viking, 1979.

America's Quilts and Coverlets by Carleton L. Safford and Robert Bishop, Weathervane Books, 1980.

Quilts Their Story and How to Make Them by Marie D. Webster, Doubleday, 1928.

The Pieced Quilt by Jonathan Holstein, New York Graphic Society, 1973.

The Denver Art Museum Quilts and Coverlets by Imelda DeGraw, Denver Art Museum, 1974.

Sunshine and Shadow, The Amish and Their Quilts, by Phyllis Haders, The Main Street Press, 1976.

The Quilt Digest by Kiracofe and Kile, San Francisco, Volume 1, 1983; Volume 2, 1984.

Kentucky Quilts 1800-1900, Introduction and quilt commentaries by Jonathan Holstein, historical text by John Finley, The Kentucky Quilt Project, 1982.

If you want more patterns for flower quilts, or need basic quilting directions, try the following sources.

Prize Country Quilts by Mary Elizabeth Johnson, Oxmoor House, Inc. 1977.

Lap Quilting with Georgia Bonesteel, Oxmoor House, Inc. 1982.

Quilts of America by Erica Wilson, Oxmoor House, Inc. 1979.

Award Winning Quilts by Effie Chalmers Pforr, Oxmoor House, Inc. 1974.

Suppliers

You can also obtain many quilting supplies by mail. Write for the name of your nearest retailer of Stearns & Foster quilt patterns, quilt batting, and other products to:

Mountain Mist Quilt Center
The Stearns & Foster Company
Cincinnati, Ohio 45215

For quilt kits, frames, and other supplies, write for a catalog to:

Lee Wards
Elgin, Ohio
and to:
Yours Truly, Inc.
P.O. Box 80218
Atlanta, Georgia 30366

For information about their batting and their contests, as well as your nearest retailer of **POLY-FIL** products, write to:

Fairfield Processing Corporation
88 Rose Hill Avenue
P.O. Drawer 1157
Danbury, Connecticut 06810

Index

Contributors

Following are some very special people who made significant contributions to *A Garden of Quilts* by lending so many of their quilts for photography and study. The designers and quilters *produce* the quilts, and the collectors help to *preserve* them and to establish a value. Each is vital to the health and future of quilting!

The Designers

Martha Skelton has been quilting since she was fifteen years old, even through the years when it seemed no one else was doing it. It was part of her family's activities—her mother, grandmothers, aunts, cousins, sisters, and neighbors as well. She says she assumed that everyone learned to make quilts the same way—firsthand from someone close by. Eventually she entered her work in local fairs, won ribbons, and now she organizes the State Quilting Bee in Jackson, Mississippi, every year! She has been a Demonstrating Craftsman at the Mississippi Arts Festival, The Craftsman's Guild of Mississippi, and when Mississippi was the featured state at the Smithsonian Festival of American Folklife in Washington, D.C., she was the featured quilter! Her work is in the permanent collection of the Stearns & Foster Company. She teaches and belongs to several quilt guilds. In her words, "Quilting can be as sociable, as solitary, as creative, as challenging, as demanding as any craft I can think of. It is certainly never boring, and is a never-ending source of interest. There is always yet another quilt I've just got to make!"

Mary Frances Owensby: At 90 years of age, Mrs. Owensby is probably our oldest contributor who is still actively quilting. She was taught to quilt by her mother who had been taught by *her* mother. She grew up in northern Missouri, but has spent most of her adult life in Linden, Alabama, where she still enters quilt shows!

Rubena Boyington, Winnie Garner, Beulah Wigley: A mother and her two daughters carry on a family tradition with their quilts. Mrs. Boyington was a third generation quilter. Taught by her mother, she made her first quilt when she was nine years old. She made only utilitarian quilts until the 1940s because she was simultaneously raising eight children and working beside her husband in the fields near Robertsdale, Alabama. After her children were grown, she had more leisure time, and began sewing very complicated quilt kits. The daughters remember watching her quilt, but it took the quilt revival of the 70s to get everybody together. Beulah has a twin sister, Beatrice, who makes fabulous pictorial quilts, using greeting cards as inspiration. There is another sister, Faye, who quilts, as well as a sister-in-law, Patty Cox Wilcox, who comes from a long line of Kentucky quilters. This family has a truly impressive body of work, and has been written about in several different quilting magazines.

The Collectors

Rick and Mary Grunbaum's interest in quilts began when they lived in New York, with the purchase of an 1860 "Princess Feather." Mary had just finished getting a degree in art at Rutgers—Rick was a photographer working at the United Nations. The interest in quilting meshed the two careers; Mary began collecting and selling old quilts as well as designing and marketing new ones, while Rick documented with his photography both the quilts and many of the women who made them. They spent two years traveling across the United States and Europe selling quilts and quilt products. Finally in 1975 they opened The Great American Coverup retail store in Dallas. With an inventory of fine antique quilts, new and custom quilts, as well as supplies and classes, they built a business which continues to thrive.

Robert Cargo was given a family quilt by his grandparents one Christmas in the 1950s, and from that beginning has accumulated one of the finest collections of quilts in Alabama. Dr. Cargo and his wife, Helen, have helped to mount shows of Alabama quilts at the Museums of Art in Birmingham and Montgomery, and many of their quilts have been featured in quilt and craft magazines as well as books about quilts. Although his primary occupation is professor of French at the University of Alabama, Dr. Cargo's passion for quilts is making him much sought after as a writer, lecturer, and reviewer of books on the subject.

In addition to those designers, collectors and quilters whose work appears on these pages, I would like to thank the following people, without whose help and support this project could not have been accomplished.

Two seminal shows provided inspiration and affirmation for this book: A Patchwork Garden, sponsored by The Hunter Museum of Art in Chattanooga, Tennessee, and The Arrowmont School of Arts and Crafts, Gatlinburg, Tennessee, in 1981, curated by Bets Ramsey; and Alabama Quilts at the Birmingham Museum of Art, curated by Gail Andrews Trechsel and Janet Strain McDonald in 1982.

For helping with photographs: Violet Boone and daughter Tony, Donald McKinley, Julia Norman, Mark Dunnam, Dottie Dunnam, Tom Bailey, Sherry Allen, Mrs. Paul Hybart, Mr. and Mrs. Nick Hare, Jo Ann Cox, Frankie McClendon, Kathel Griffin.

For finding quilts: Dot Hancock, Bette Kirkham, Ruth Chapaan, Ann Fentress, Charlotte Hagood, Flavin Glover, Lois Lang, Hazel Carter, Doris Hoover, Mary Manning, Katherine Holmes, Susanne Johnson, Sherry Allen.

For tracing patterns: Debbie Black, Pat Holland, Cathy Holland, Laura Holland, Betty Smotherman, Wallace Johnson, Julia Norman, Susanne Johnson.

For technical information and loaning photographs: Janet Dreiling; Barbara Brackman; Questa Benberry, Jo Ann Cox, Marti Michell, Bryce and Donna Hamilton, Jean Wittig.

For typing: Polly Stabler, Kathy McNeece, Russ Sirmon, Elizabeth Johnson, Kay Johnson.

Editor: Linda Baltzell Wright
Editorial Assistant: Lenda Wyatt
Design: David Morrison
Photography: Beth Maynor, John O'Hagan, Jim Bathie, Mac Jamieson, Sylvia Martin, Bob Lancaster, Bruce Roberts, David Mathews, Henry French, Brian Blouser, Nancy Halpern, Jack L. Hoover
Art: Diana Smith, Teresa Ray, David Morrison
Art Director: Bob Nance
Production: Jerry Higdon, Jane Bonds, Jim Thomas

158